Margaret Cooling is the author of over 40 books on RE and assemblies and two books for youth groups. For many years her speciality has been in using the arts to communicate Christianity within the field of education. She has worked with both the National Gallery Company and the BBC on this. Margaret preaches and writes drama and Bible study material. Over the years she has been involved in youth work, Sunday school, leading house groups, quiet days and a retreat. Margaret has taught in both primary and secondary schools. For the last 18 years she has been engaged in writing and training across the UK and in Australia. She trains both teachers and clergy to work in schools. In the past few years Margaret has begun to adapt her experience and knowledge within the field of education to work with churches. For several years she ran an education unit for a theological college and provided in-service training for the staff of Spurgeon's College. She runs training days for church leaders to work within different areas of the church.

Published by
The Bible Reading Fellowship
First Floor, Elsfield Hall
15–17 Elsfield Way, Oxford OX2 8FG
Website: www.brf.org.uk

ISBN 1 84101 347 1
First published 2005
10 9 8 7 6 5 4 3 2 1 0
All rights reserved

Acknowledgments
Unless otherwise stated, scripture quotations are taken from the Contemporary
English Version of the Bible published by HarperCollins Publishers, copyright ©
1991, 1992, 1995 American Bible Society.

Scripture quotations taken from the Holy Bible, New International Version,
copyright © 1973, 1978, 1984 by International Bible Society, are used by
permission of Hodder & Stoughton Limited. All rights reserved. 'NIV' is a registered
trademark of International Bible Society. UK trademark number 1448790.

Extracts from the Authorized Version of the Bible (The King James Bible), the rights
in which are vested in the Crown, are reproduced by permission of the Crown's
Patentee, Cambridge University Press.

A catalogue record for this book is available from the British Library

Printed and bound in Great Britain by
Bookmarque, Croydon

Creating a learning church

Improving teaching and learning in the local church

Margaret Cooling

To Robert and Rebecca and my granddaughter,
Charlotte Jane, who is learning fast.

ACKNOWLEDGMENTS

I would like to express my thanks to the congregations of St Helen's, St Luke's and St Andrew's, who have been very patient as I have learned and experimented over the past 18 years. I would also like to express my gratitude to the following people, who have read and commented on this manuscript.

The Reverend Ben Beecroft (St Helen's, Stapleford)
The Reverend Chris Beecroft (St Helen's, Stapleford)
The Reverend Simon Helme (Dursely URC Church)
Deborah Helme (Sunday Club leader, Dursely URC Church)
Diane Hudson (Christian Aid organizer, prison visitor St Andrew's, Mottingham)
Ewan Jones (Assistant youth worker, St Matthew's, Cheltenham)
George Oliver (Reader and housegroup leader, St Helen's, Stapleford)
Meg Oliver (Sunday Club and housegroup leader, St Helen's, Stapleford)
Jayne Seward (Sunday Club leader, St Matthew's, Cheltenham)
Carolyn Tennant (Children's and youth worker, Leckhampton Baptist)
The Reverend Timothy Watson (formerly St Matthew's, Cheltenham)

Contents

SECTION FOUR: EMOTIONS AND LEARNING

SECTION FIVE: LEARNING AND DIFFERENCE

SECTION SIX: REMEMBERING WHAT WE HAVE LEARNED

SECTION SEVEN: MOVING ON

Foreword

It has taken a surprisingly long time for some of us to realize that just because you know something, it does not mean you also know how to communicate it. But now even the world of Higher Education, in which I work and which is a bit slow about these things, has begun seriously to grapple with the self-evident dictum that 'nobody has taught anything until somebody has learnt something'. To give priority to the process of learning puts the work of teaching in a new light.

The old assumption in the formal education system was that possessing a qualification in a subject qualified you to teach it. It was certainly true that many possessed a natural flair for communication and teaching. Instinctively they knew what 'worked' and, by their enthusiasm for their subject, they carried others along. But all of us along the way have also experienced what it is like when others, who may well have been experts in their field, simply had no idea of how to stimulate learning. How people learn has become a field of study in its own right, and a fascinating one at that; and knowing how people learn should help those of us called to teach to fulfil our task more effectively.

Margaret Cooling's book is designed primarily for those who teach and learn in the life of the church. In producing it she has drawn upon a rich and varied background as an enabler of learning. I can testify from personal experience that the material contained in this book will open up new perspectives and stimulate new approaches for any group which understands itself as a community of learning.

There are few more satisying human experiences than that of discovery—discovering things for ourselves and watching others do the same. This is what learning and teaching involve, and this book is directed towards that end.

Dr Nigel G. Wright
Principal, Spurgeon's College, London

Introduction

WHAT THIS BOOK AIMS TO DO

What we hope to learn and what we actually learn are often two different things. For most of us there is a gap between teaching and learning. This book is about closing that gap and creating a learning church where everybody embarks on a journey of learning with God that is not only lifelong but also life-changing. This book is only an introduction to how we learn; it does not cover everything. This book covers:

- Learning, what it is and how we plan for it
- What stops people from learning
- How we can become better learners
- How the brain works when we learn
- How to teach and learn in a way that works with the way we are created
- Strategies for closing the gap between teaching and learning
- Examples of the strategies in practice in sermons, youth work, Sunday club, children's talks, drama, reflections, prayers, quiet days, Bible reading and Bible studies

Each chapter gives basic information, followed by discussion of what it means in practice in the church and at least one detailed example. At the back of the book (p. 192) you will find an action plan. You might like to turn to it now and consider it as you read further.

On completing the book, you may feel that it confirms many of the things that you already do, but you should also be able to locate areas where you can improve your own teaching and learning. These areas will be different for each individual.

RESEARCH

The last 20 years have been a time of great discovery. Much of what scientists understand about the human brain has been discovered in that time. Many of the discoveries are only just beginning to influence what people do, but they have the potential to make an enormous impact on all areas of teaching and learning. Over a longer period, there has also been a lot of research into how people learn, and this too is influencing practice.

Guidelines, not rules

This book draws on the results of studies concerning how we learn, and tries to apply them to the church. As in any field, however, experts differ, and the way research is interpreted and applied varies. For example, scientists and researchers ask very specific questions about the workings of the brain and learning, but we need to ask very general ones and apply the answers in different situations. The result is not an equation—'do this and success is guaranteed'— human beings are more complex than that. However, the book suggests a range of strategies for improving teaching and learning. I have selected insights that have 'chimed' with my experience and that of others over the years. Please treat them as guidelines, not unbreakable rules.

An important note

It is possible to get the learning strategy right and find that learning still does not happen, because relationships are wrong (although an emphasis on right relationships is part of the learning strategy). It cannot be emphasized enough that learning takes place within relationships; relationships are of paramount importance. It is also important to remember that not everything has to be in place for learning to happen—only some factors—so don't feel overwhelmed. We don't have to do everything at once!

HEALTH AND SAFETY

In all activities, health and safety must be borne in mind. For example, when lighting candles, always stand them in damp sand. You should refer to your own church's health and safety documents.

THE FRAMEWORK OF FAITH

This is a book about rethinking how we learn. It explores a number of strategies and techniques for improving learning. However, details are not included on how we pray or rely on God and the work of the Holy Spirit; that is the assumed framework within which all teaching and learning takes place.

Although this 'framework of faith' is assumed, that does not mean that it is not given priority. The primary purpose of this book is to explore strategies for learning, but faith is integral to the book and is woven through it. This should become clear through the worked examples at the end of each chapter.

Certain faith issues are crucial to learning:

- *A relationship with God that is marked by growth and change:* Learning is about growth and change. A person who has a relationship with God that is not open to change cannot learn (2 Peter 3:18). An active and growing relationship is essential if learning is going to be of God and not just about God.
- *An openness to God:* Learning is also about openness. Sometimes we have trouble learning because what we learn doesn't fit our preconceived ideas, as the apostle Peter discovered (Acts 10). God is full of surprises. This book is about attitudes to learning that allow us to respond to those surprises.
- *Good relationships with other Christians:* Learning works best in relationships. We need to learn from each other. We can bounce ideas off each other and encourage each other to learn. We can

draw strength from others. We can support each other if what we learn makes us feel 'wobbly' until we have worked it through. Together, we work through ideas and apply them (Philippians 3:17). Finally, we live out our learning in communities. Learning is not an individual activity to increase brain power; it is a lively engagement with knowledge that is personal and active, and can change the way we live out our relationship with God in the world.

- *A willingness to see teaching and learning as co-operation with the Holy Spirit:* Sometimes strategies for learning are seen as negating the work of the Holy Spirit: after all, Jesus said that he would send the Holy Spirit, who would lead us into truth and understanding (John 14:25–26). Isaiah 55:11 says that the word of the Lord will accomplish its purpose, so why do we need to learn about learning? Surely the Holy Spirit will do it all? In no way do adequate preparation and good learning strategies deny the work of the Holy Spirit. The techniques in this book try to work with the way that God made us (as far as we can know that). It is about working with the Spirit in order to be a channel through which the message can flow, by removing obstacles to learning. God graciously allows us to share in this creative work.
- *A faith that integrates prayer, worship and learning:* Prayer and worship are part of the way in which we become open to God and enabled to learn. They are not an 'add-on' but a vital part of our learning process.
- *A belief that God made us 'whole':* In Western thinking, we tend to divide people up into body, mind, emotions and spirit—although this attitude is changing and we are beginning to think more holistically. In the Bible, people are viewed as a whole. Just as we worship with body, mind and spirit (Deuteronomy 6:5), so we learn in that way.

Getting started

CHAPTER 1

Our amazing ability to learn

God has made each of us unique. Members of a church congregation vary in age, education and life experience. They also vary in another important way: each of their brains is unique. Like fingerprints, no two brains are the same. Not only are they unique, they are amazingly designed:

- A developing baby gains a quarter of a million brain cells a day.
- This results in a multi-trillion network of connections in the brain that is capable of doing 20 million billion calculations a second.
- The brain can send messages at speeds of up to 150mph.
- The retina of the eye is only as thick as a sheet of paper, yet it can distinguish up to eight million shades of colour.

In the words of the psalmist, we are created in a wonderful way (Psalm 139:14).

God has given us a brain that is extremely versatile and can process information in many different ways: it can analyse and be creative; it can solve problems and imagine. We probably use only a small part of its potential.

People used to think that intelligence was fixed by what we inherited from our parents. However, research has thrown doubts on this idea. Intelligence is not completely determined by what we inherit; it can be modified. This means that we can improve.

WHO IS THE TEACHER? WHO IS THE LEARNER?

The answer to this question is 'everyone'. Once, teaching and learning were rigidly divided roles. Now, we are more aware that we are all lifelong learners. Different people may take on the role of teacher, even if it is for a short period and in an informal manner. Even those with the designated role of 'teacher' are part of a learning community and should see themselves as part of a communal journey of discovery. It's all a question of attitudes.

The church is not the place for an 'expert' to impart their knowledge to the congregation, who are regarded as 'empty' and in need of filling. Expertise matters, there are gifts of teaching that should be fostered and used, but experts also need to learn from others. The congregation have their own expertise to share: they are not 'empty vessels'.

We differ in lots of ways as learners—for example, in personality, and in how abstractly or concretely we think. It is important to bear in mind that space allows for only a few of these differences to be followed up in this book.

WHAT DOES THIS MEAN IN PRACTICE?

If intelligence can be modified, then how we teach and learn becomes very important. There are a number of factors that affect learning:

- *Attitudes:* A 'can do' attitude helps. How we think about ourselves, and what others think about our ability to learn, are crucial. Negative attitudes, such as 'I'm too old to learn' or 'I've nothing to offer', 'I'm scared of learning' or 'Learning is too much like hard work', hinder learning. Such attitudes may be the result of bad past experiences in the education system or the church, personality factors or sin. There are no easy answers to negative attitudes, but they can be changed over time as confidence and good relationships are built up.

- *Independence:* We need to be learners who know how to get hold of the information we require. Too often we become over-dependent on others. That degree of dependence should be on God, not teachers (1 Corinthians 3:1–7).
- *Resilience:* We need to be resilient learners who do not give up if we don't understand immediately. We need to 'go on with God', not fall at the first hurdle. We can do this by encouraging each other and by our attitudes to 'mistakes'. Mistakes in understanding can be things from which we learn, not disasters. If we are in leadership roles, we need to set an example in resilient learning, which means admitting when we don't understand or when we get things wrong, while showing that we are still committed to learning.
- *Recognition that the skills of learning and teaching don't come automatically:* It is sometimes assumed that we know instinctively how to learn or that having the gift of teaching or preaching means we don't have to learn about communication. Of course, some learning does come naturally, but not all. The Holy Spirit does give gifts of teaching (Romans 12:4–7), but we are required to work with him. If we think that all learning just 'happens', we tend to concentrate on the content and pay little attention to communication.

SOME THINGS TO THINK ABOUT

Think about what it is like to be on the receiving end of teaching and preaching. If we preach or teach, we need to imagine what it feels like to sit through one of our own sermons, Bible studies, youth group or Sunday club sessions. Ask yourself the following questions:

- What is my attitude to learning?
- Have I ever looked at how I learn?
- Are there training or refresher courses I could consider?
- Do we share our talents and training?

- Are my talents fostered?
- Do we as a church train preachers as preachers and teachers as teachers? (The skills are not the same.) Have I considered if I have skills in these areas?

An outline of a training day session on deep and surface learning and barriers to learning

This outline draws on material from Chapters 2 and 4, as well as the one you have just read. It will need to be adapted, depending on who the participants are. The times given are approximate.

A ONE-AND-A-HALF-HOUR SESSION

Introduction and worship (12 minutes)

Put a *very brief* overview of what will be happening during the session on a flipchart. Share the objective with the group, which is: **'To understand what deep learning is, the barriers to it and how some of these might be overcome.'**

Put the facts about our amazing ability to learn, from page 16, on an OHP or PowerPoint. Use them to lead into worship and praise.

Talk (10 minutes)

Explain deep and surface learning (see pages 23–24). Introduce the levels of learning using an OHP or PowerPoint. Give an example for each type of learning, and ask group members to supply others.

Activity (5 minutes)

Put the examples of surface learning, from pages 26–27, on separate cards. Repeat with the deep learning examples from the same pages, using a different coloured card. Ask people to match them into pairs.

Group activity (5 minutes)

Enlarge and photocopy the examples of levels of learning on pages 28–29 but 'white out' the levels on a master copy before you do this. Cut up the photocopy so that the examples are separated. Assign a letter to each example, then Blu-Tack the examples around the room. Ask people to move around the room, find an example for each level and write down its letter.

Summary (12 minutes)

Bring the group back together and share your results. Together, sum up the differences between the levels of learning and how we distinguish between surface and deep learning. Discuss ways in which these levels of learning can be incorporated into the church's teaching and learning.

Talk (3 minutes)

Introduce the idea of barriers to learning (pages 36–38).

Whole group activity (20 minutes)

Put the factors that create barriers to learning on to cards and Blu-Tack them up where everyone can see them (on a wall). As a whole group, sort them into 'sets' of related factors (for example, factors about feelings would make a set). You may prefer to have headings for sets (for example, doctrine, attitudes/ways of thinking, feeling) already prepared and displayed on different coloured card. People can then come and move the factor cards, putting them under the appropriate headings as the discussion progresses. Each small group can then take a set and discuss ways of overcoming some of the barriers within it.

Plenary (10–15 minutes)

Bring the groups back together and ask them to share some of their suggestions for ways of overcoming barriers.

Bring the session to a close by summing up what has been learned, and return to the objective. Has it been achieved?

Ask everyone to share with the person next to them something important that they will take from the day.

CHAPTER 2

What do we mean by 'learn'?

Learning can mean different things to different people, and can work on different levels. Learning can be:

- *Level one:* More information, facts and memorizing.
- *Level two:* Discovering personal challenges and meaning.
- *Level three:* Interpreting information (working out its meaning) in order to understand ourselves, others, God and the world differently.
- *Level four:* Integrating what we have learned into our lives in the way we think, feel and act.

The first level is often known as 'surface' learning. It sticks with 'facts' and is more interested in breadth than depth. Surface learning tends to reproduce information. The other levels are often called 'deep' learning because they go beneath the surface of information to its meaning and significance. 'Deep' learning is about understanding, relating knowledge to our own experience, recognizing patterns and principles and interacting with knowledge, allowing it to affect us as well as working on it. The two types of learning are in competition only if surface learning is seen as the end result rather than as the stepping stone for deeper learning.

Learning in the Bible means far more than learning facts. The Hebrew word, *yada*, that is often translated 'know' covers factual knowledge but also means close personal experience and encounter —hence the old KJV translation of Genesis 4:1, '... and Adam knew his wife Eve'. *Yada* is not just knowledge *about* God; it is knowledge *of* God. It goes beyond information to meaning, beyond facts to understanding and experience that changes our lives. This does not mean, of course, that we do not need information: it is essential if our understanding is to have depth and it is the foundation on which we build.

Too often, however, in the church, we see learning as just putting more information in our heads, when what we really need is help to find meaning in the Bible and help to discover new ways of seeing God and the world and letting them change our lives. We cannot assume that this will just happen. Whenever we split learning into several parts (information, meaning, application), we reduce our ability to learn. Discovering meaning and applying it to our lives helps us to learn information because we tend to remember what we put into practice, so we should think of the different levels of learning as woven together rather than as separate threads.

In the church, we are not in the business of collecting information for information's sake. We need to remind ourselves constantly that we learn for a purpose—to know God and grow in a relationship with him. Bearing that purpose in mind, we should select information for teaching and preaching on a 'need to know' basis.

In this book, the word 'learning' usually refers to 'deep learning'.

WHAT DOES THIS MEAN IN PRACTICE?

We need to think about how we plan. Often, if we are asked to plan a series for a Bible study or holiday club, we look at the information we want to pass on and parcel it out into sections that will fit the time allocated. We could do it differently, however.

• We could read a Bible passage and locate the personal challenges, saying to ourselves, 'How could this passage challenge us or help us to see God and the world differently? How could it change our lives (thinking, feeling and action)?'

- When we have located these challenges, they can be used to drive our planning. The challenge identified should determine the questions we ask, the stories we tell, the activities we plan, the music, the issues for discussion and the way we structure a session.
- We can set goals that aim for deep learning.

WHY IS DEEP LEARNING DIFFICULT?

There are a number of reasons why deep learning is difficult. Some of the reasons are noted below, and are also followed up elsewhere in this book.

- Sometimes we feel very dull and 'flat'. It's hard to break out of that feeling, to become excited about the Bible and find personal meaning in it.
- We are imperfect people. We have been redeemed, but our process of sanctification is ongoing. As Christians, God is working on us; we are not finished products. As such, it is not surprising that we often find that we have to work at praying and engaging with the Bible. The fact that we are imperfect still plays its part in hindering learning.
- The brain has millions of cells that connect to create pathways. Learning happens when a new connection is made. We tend to use old, well-worn pathways of thought rather than creating new ones by thinking something through for ourselves or thinking differently. Imagine the brain as a forest. It's easier to walk down a well-trodden pathway rather than hacking out a new one.

Deep and surface learning

Below is a selection of examples of the distinction between deep and surface learning.

Surface: I can retell some of the parables about the kingdom, such as the mustard seed and the hidden treasure (Matthew 13:31–32 and 44).
Deep: I understand that the kingdom came with Jesus but will not come fully until he returns. We live in the in-between times (somewhere between heaven and the supermarket), living out our daily, often humdrum lives, in the light of what is now and what is to be.

Surface: I know the story of Christmas from both Luke's and Matthew's Gospels, and I can list the similarities and differences between them.
Deep: I understand that God came to earth at Christmas. He lived a life like mine, knowing what it feels like to laugh and to cry, to be lonely and tired, to be loved and feel joy. When I pray, he understands.

Surface: I can follow Paul's argument in Romans 8.
Deep: When I read Romans 8, it changes the way I see myself in relation to God and how I feel about myself.

Surface: I know the names of all the books of the Bible and can recite them in chronological order.
Deep: I understand the message of the Bible, the 'big story' of God's salvation and what it means for me and the world.

Surface: I know the story of Shadrach, Meshach and Abednego in the fiery furnace and scholars' debates about its authenticity.
Deep: I understand that God does not always rescue us from danger but he is always there with us in the danger, as he was in the fire with Shadrach, Meshach and Abednego.

Surface: I know the background to the letter of 1 Corinthians.
Deep: Paul's advice to the Corinthian church challenges me to show more love in my life.

Surface: I can read Genesis 1—3 in the original Hebrew.
Deep: Genesis 1—3 helps me to see the world as good, but not now as God intended. It helps me to see people as made in the image of God, even if that image is spoilt. It changes the way I treat people. They all deserve to be treated with respect, and so do I.

Different levels of learning

The following is a selection of examples of the distinction between different levels of learning.

Level one

- I can recite the Ten Commandments.

- I can retell the story of Moses' and the Israelites' escape from Egypt.

- I know the original Greek words for 'love'.

Level two

- I know that serving God is more than keeping 'rules'. He challenges me to love him with my heart and mind and body (Deuteronomy 6:5).

- The story of Moses challenges me to believe in a compassionate God, a God of justice who cares for the oppressed.

- I understand that God's love is better than the love of the best parent I can imagine.

Level three

- Serving God with my whole being affects how I think and act. What I do with my mind and body matters.

- Knowing that God is a God of justice, who cares for the oppressed, affects how I think about current affairs.

- Knowing that I am adopted by God, and that nothing can separate me from his love, changes how I feel and think about myself and how I see others.

Level four

- I look for opportunities to serve God with my mind and body as well as my feelings. I no longer just try to keep the rules.

- I look for opportunities to bring about justice in our world. It's only small, but I've started a Fair Trade stall at church.

- Knowing that I am loved by God changes how I live. Feeling secure in God's love, I am free to reach out to others. I've spent more time at work listening to colleagues.

CHAPTER 3

How do we know when learning has happened?

Biologically, when any learning happens, connections are made between brain cells and this creates pathways. Unfortunately we cannot see this happening. There are, however, some possible pointers to learning taking place—though no guarantees. Learning (to various degrees) may have taken place when people can do the following:

- *Use information:* When we can take what we have learned and use it, change its form or make it part of a creative process, we can probably be said to know it.
- *Sum up or explain:* If we can summarize information without distorting it, or explain its significance to someone else (not just repeat it), it's a good indication that learning has happened.
- *Make deductions, predict, connect or apply:* Learning has probably taken place when we can work out what something means for us as a Christian, how it will affect other aspects of life and and how it can be applied to daily living. That means making connections between work, family life, leisure, the wider world and our faith. It also means connecting the various aspects of our faith, such as worship, prayer and the Bible. When this occurs, learning has probably happened.
- *Locate what is important and evaluate:* Learning is indicated when we show the ability to find what is important in a text or a situation, and when we can weigh up information and evaluate its importance for us.

- *Spot problems and possibilities and create questions:* When we can spot problems and possibilities for ourselves as Christians and can create questions based on what we have learned, it suggests that learning has taken place.

All of the above encourage deep learning. They do not stop at information gathering; they proceed to meaning, significance and application.

WHAT DOES THIS MEAN IN PRACTICE?

Encouraging deep learning to take place sometimes means changing priorities in the church so that this type of learning is valued. Some practical suggestions follow.

Shift the emphasis

In all church contexts, move from an emphasis on information to an emphasis on meaning and application. This may mean taking a new look at material used in Sunday club and youth work, and retraining staff where necessary. It means looking at Bible studies and sermons and making the change of emphasis plain to all involved in running them.

Create an arena

If we are asking questions or coming up with problems and possibilities, we might have grasped something very important and need an arena to hammer out the issues that are concerning us. Often it's difficult to find someone to talk things over with. In some churches, if people with similar concerns get together they are labelled as a 'clique' and viewed with suspicion. Alan Jamieson, in his book *A Churchless Faith* (SPCK, 2002), explored the faith of people who leave the church. He found that the 'leavers' were often faithful, thoughtful people who had been in positions of leadership for many years. Many felt that they could not explore their faith issues within the church, and left.

The type of arenas that churches create will differ according to their situation. Even a change of attitude helps. One example might be to see more church book circles, where groups commit themselves to reading a book over a month or two and then come together to discuss the issues raised. Different groups could choose different books according to interest and level of challenge.

Make opportunities

We need opportunities to express our newfound understanding—perhaps through art, discussion, poetry, presentation, prayer, dance, drama or music, or whatever is appropriate. Some of us like working with the creative arts; others can't think of anything worse. Some people prefer to contribute to a discussion, give a short explanation, create a chart, contribute a comment to a display, do a presentation or just share during a service.

Create a safe environment

We need a climate in which it is all right to evaluate information, follow a train of thought or hammer out the consequences of understanding in daily life, rather than always being told the answer. We need to be allowed to follow a line of thought without necessarily having an emotional investment in it. We often 'try things on for size' or just want to see where an idea leads, and then draw back from it once we have thought through the implications. Sometimes, that freedom to explore is discouraged or we are seen as 'wedded' to an idea when we are only exploring it. When that happens, there is no way of stepping back without considerable loss of face.

Stay cool

We need to rejoice if we are learning and growing as a church, but be prepared for some challenging and exciting situations. We will not necessarily agree with each other and we will need to cultivate respect, humility and patience. How we talk to and think about each other matters: there is a place for old-fashioned grace and decency. Richard Mouw's book *Uncommon Decency* (IVP, 1992) is very insightful.

Activities that may show evidence of learning

If we are able to do some of the following *types* of activities, learning may have taken place.

USING INFORMATION

- Read Psalm 13 and change it into a personal prayer.
- Read Psalm 100 and create a dance to accompany the reading of the psalm in a service, or create a banner design based on the psalm for church.
- Read Proverbs 15:1 and think of situations where this principle can be applied to life as a Christian.

SUMMING UP OR EXPLAINING

- Summarize or explain 1 Timothy 3:1–12.
- Summarize or explain 1 Corinthians 15.
- Summarize or explain Psalm 46.

MAKING DEDUCTIONS, PREDICTING, CONNECTING OR APPLYING

- Work out (deduce) what Philippians 4:4–7 means for our Christian lives. Does it mean we should always be smiling and happy?
- Predict the neighbours' response to Zacchaeus' returning the money he had swindled (Luke 19:1–9).

- Say what connects Psalm 23, the parable of the lost sheep (Luke 15:4–7), John 10:1–18 and Good Friday worship?
- Apply the advice from Paul in Galatians 6:1–10 to church life. What would it mean?

LOCATING WHAT IS IMPORTANT AND EVALUATING

- Read Jeremiah 1. Locate a significant sentence and say why it is significant for you.
- Read Micah 6:8. Why do you think this is often considered to be a key verse?

SPOTTING PROBLEMS AND POSSIBILITIES AND CREATING QUESTIONS

- Read 1 Corinthians 10:23—11:1. What is the relevance of this passage for today's living? Are there possible problems? What are the possibilities? What questions would we want to ask?

CHAPTER 4

What stops us learning?

There are a number of things that can stop learning from taking place. A few have already been mentioned, but further factors have been grouped below under two headings. Read through the lists and think through your own situation. This list does not deal with physical barriers to learning such as impairment or the age of the learner.

These insights draw on the work of John Hull in *What Prevents Christian Adults from Learning?* (SCM Press, 1985) as well as other scholars. Although Hull's analysis has been used here, agreement with all his conclusions is not implied.

Learning is difficult if we:

- think that learning is only for the intelligent.
- think that we don't have to deal with our own imperfections in relation to learning. Learning involves the will and the mind. Factors such as laziness, arrogance and pride can all inhibit learning.
- think that learning is for children and school.
- allow our curiosity to be dulled. Curiosity is one of the main engines for learning.
- keep faith and thinking in separate mental boxes.
- think that learning is a low-status activity (and that teaching is high-status).
- think that the church is only a haven, a place to come for refreshment, not a place to be challenged to learn.

- feel insecure in belief, thinking, 'If I start probing or learning, it may disturb my faith or make it fall apart.'
- feel apathetic and dull due to emotional and physical factors.
- resist learning and growing because we don't want to go any further, and simply defend the stage we are at.
- fear being wrong: some of us get nervous when it comes to contributing to a discussion.
- fear change: learning means change for Christians.
- are determined to be vague, thinking, 'If I am definite about my beliefs, I might have to live up to them or I will leave them open to being disproved—better to stay vague.'
- view things that come through the senses as distractions rather than as opportunities to learn. This cuts down learning, as we often learn through our senses.
- think there is no need to learn because we are absolutely sure that we are right.
- think that the way we (in our church) understand or do things is the only way to understand and do things—believing that we have nothing to learn from others.
- see learning *merely* as a way of satisfying our needs and think that once the need is satisfied we don't have to learn any more— saying, for example, 'I need to know just enough of the Bible to teach in Sunday club.'
- believe that if we have faith we don't need to learn.

Learning is difficult when the church:

- over-stresses the individual: we learn best in relationships. When people know and respect each other, they are more willing to listen to what others have to say, whether in informal groups or in more formal teaching and preaching situations.
- over-emphasizes authority and passively accepting information rather than genuine learning.
- too strongly stresses certain doctrines, or those doctrines are misunderstood by the congregation. This can include ideas such

as 'God has a plan for our lives', which can be misunderstood as 'We don't need to do anything; God will do it all.'

- retreats into an unnecessarily rigid framework of beliefs and feels threatened by the many beliefs present in our plural world (including other forms of Christianity). For example, some people will only read books published by a certain publisher.
- focuses on the past rather than the present and future. Learning is about moving forward on the foundation of the past.
- sets up an 'ideal Christian adult'—for example, 'a person of simple faith'. This may be unconscious, but the 'ideal' or 'average' acts as a magnet and people gravitate towards it.
- feels threatened by a learning congregation. The church may have a vested interest in people not growing beyond a certain point (for example, because they are easier to live with).
- sees learning as controlled rather than enabled by the teacher.
- goes for uniformity and tries to turn everyone into the same type of Christian.

WHAT DOES THIS MEAN IN PRACTICE?

There is no IQ test for the kingdom of heaven. We all have some learning potential, although it will vary. Learning involves the mind, emotions and action; it is not just for the big-brained. Teachers should help learning rather than control it, creating people who can learn on their own and with others.

Our fear of learning is real and should be acknowledged. Learning does create discomfort; it can make us rethink cherished beliefs learned as a child. Even if beliefs such as 'God will always protect us' and 'the good will always prosper' do not work in the real world, we are often reluctant to let them go. Learning, however, can also relieve discomfort. When our beliefs are 'not working', learning can relieve distress. Does the Bible really say that God will always protect us or that the good always prosper? Read 2 Timothy 3:12. Learning can bring our faith and reality into line.

Accepting the authority of the Bible or the church does not have to inhibit learning; it is a matter of emphasis and how authority is handled. Yes, the Bible is authoritative, but our understanding of it is not. We grow and learn and develop in our understanding. Learning and authority can go hand in hand.

We can learn from the past. Our traditions can enrich our present Christian lives but tradition should not be a ball and chain. The founders of many Christian traditions were people who refused to be bound by the past themselves—Luther, Calvin and Wesley being good examples.

Just as travel broadens the mind, so pluralism (the existence of people who think and act differently) can help us to learn. We don't have to agree with them but it can help us to break out of complacency, thinking that we have nothing to learn.

Humility is a Christian virtue and essential to learning (1 Peter 5:5). We might be 'right' over certain issues but we won't be perfect in understanding: we can all learn. Most of us long for certainty and there is nothing wrong with that. Learning can contribute to certainty, although we will always have to live with a degree of ambiguity in this life for we only know in part (1 Corinthians 13:12). Mystery is part of our faith. There are some things that only God knows, but we can be confident that we can know enough for salvation. Faith and learning are not in competition. Learning can be 'faith seeking understanding'. It is our attitude that is all-important.

Deliberate vagueness will be challenged by learning. Learning often has a twin effect: it clarifies some areas and shows us the complexities of others. In either case, it challenges our behaviour. Church was never meant to be the religious equivalent of a hot bath. Stimulation and challenge can be as refreshing as relaxation.

If we see learning as only good for satisfying needs, then once that need is satisfied we may think that we don't need to learn any more. (It's a bit like buying a chocolate bar when you are hungry: why eat another when your hunger is satisfied?) Learning does satisfy our needs, but learning should be something that attracts us forward into growth as a Christian—a growth that never ends in this life.

We can use various tactics to inhibit learning:

- avoidance: making sure we do not get into a learning situation
- distraction: focusing on social activities, the building—anything but learning
- distortion: what people say and what others hear can be quite different
- filtering: we can all develop selective deafness

Curiosity is the driving force in learning, so it is something that must be cultivated. Too often, our curiosity is quenched. We need to keep curiosity alive and to keep asking questions about our faith.

Overcoming barriers to learning

1. Invite people from different Christian traditions to share their perspective. This can open up new ways of seeing things while we remain in our own traditions.

2. Draw on insights from other traditions when teaching or learning. Remember, something is not wrong just because a person we normally disagree with says it's right.

3. Communicate messages about the status of learning by being willing to both give and receive teaching as appropriate.

4. The example set by the leadership is crucial. Do leaders feel threatened when people grow? Are they prepared to answer questions and explore issues if asked?

5. We react better if new ideas are introduced in a way that allows us to consider them. If a new idea is presented in a way that immediately challenges our previous ideas, we tend to reject it. We need new ideas presented in a way that gives us the freedom to consider them without feeling either that we *must* take them on board (to please the leader) or that we *must* reject them (in order to save face).

6. We often feel we have more freedom to consider ideas if they are presented in a way that is a little emotionally detached, or if humour is used.

7. We all need time and space to think things through. Learning doesn't have to be rushed. Ideas that seem daringly new and even shocking when they are first presented to us can feel 'old hat' after a few months.

8. We learn better if we are not overloaded and move at an appropriate pace.

9. We need teaching that is right for our age and ability level. Teaching at the wrong level makes people feel like failures, and discourages learning.

10. Manage tactfully change that results from learning (see pages 188–190).

Plans, patterns and connections

CHAPTER 5

Planning for learning

Planning for deep learning is not necessarily difficult, but it is different, and a variety of planning methods can be used. One—finding personal challenges in Bible passages—has already been discussed (p. 24). Another method is 'concept cracking'. It is not the only other method, but it is the only one explored in detail in this book.

Imagine that your church has decided to study John's Gospel for an eight-week period. In planning for this study, the most common approach is to work through the book, or to decide how much you can get through in the allotted time. An alternative way, however, is to decide what are the key themes and big ideas (concepts) and then select the material you need in order to communicate the essential truths of John's Gospel.

This approach, concept cracking, concentrates on the big ideas, as it is in these that we tend to find the meaning and challenge that enable learning to take place. This approach makes sure that the emphasis is on meaning, not just the accumulation of information.

To take an example from biology, imagine that we want to teach pupils in school about mammals. We could show them lots of mammals—elephants, mice, cats, humans, pigs and horses. Alternatively, we could tell them the characteristics of a mammal (it bears live young and suckles them, it is warm-blooded, and so on) and give them enough examples to recognize the characteristics for themselves when next they meet an animal. Concept cracking is like this latter approach.

Thinking now of John's Gospel, rather than going through the

Gospel verse by verse, we could explore it through the concept of miracles as signs pointing to who Jesus is. The concept of miracles as signs can then be used to organize the material. For example, the healing of the man born blind in John 9 can be linked to John 1:1–9. We could not organize the whole Gospel under this heading —only relevant material in manageable amounts.

The advantage of looking at one or two concepts at a time is that depth is given preference over breadth. What applies to a whole Gospel also applies to individual passages and stories. Often, a Bible passage contains half a dozen big ideas that we do not have time to explore in any depth—and just mentioning them is not enough. Concept cracking allows us to take a subject through to the highest levels of learning. It also means that we can revisit a passage many times and study it with a different concept in focus each time.

Helping people to understand the big ideas (concepts) of the Bible is like giving them a set of keys. Concept cracking gives us the freedom and independence to learn for ourselves. Once we have understood a concept (for example, 'covenant') and seen it illustrated in several passages, it unlocks many other parts of the Bible for us.

WHAT DOES THIS MEAN IN PRACTICE?

In practice, concept cracking means planning with concepts uppermost. This can be achieved by using the model 'USED' as follows:

Unpack: After prayerful study and reflection, unpack the text and list the big ideas (concepts).

Select: Select one concept from the 'Unpack' section—two related ones at the most.

Engage: Think through how to engage people so that they relate to the selected idea. How can the idea be related to experience? Use the selected idea to drive the planning and decide the illustrations, activities, music, prayers and so on.

Deliver: Think through how to deliver the material in order to bring out the meaning, encourage a thinking and feeling response, and make it applicable to daily life. When we know what to communicate, we have only done half the job. We then have to work out how we are going to communicate it.

In the 'Unpacking' stage, only list the major ideas in the text. The minor ideas can be referred to, but there may be a better biblical text in which those ideas are central.

'USED' can be used for talks, youth sessions, Bible studies and sermons. It enables people to return many times to the same text and explore it in a different way each time.

Some people ask whether they should tell only the part of the story or text relevant to the concept, or use the whole passage. Usually the whole story, text or section of text should be used, with a change of emphasis, depending on the concept being explored. It is important to respect the integrity of the text and put ideas in the context of the whole passage.

Planning a Sunday club session on Zacchaeus

UNPACK

Start planning the session by unpacking the story of Zacchaeus from Luke 19:1–10. The main concepts in the story are acceptance and rejection, repentance, change, making amends and salvation.

SELECT

For younger children (3–7s), the idea of change and how Zacchaeus changed with Jesus' help would be an appropriate single theme to select.

ENGAGE

To engage with the theme, have ready a dressing-up box. Spend a few moments showing how we can change our appearance by the way we dress. Let the children experiment too.

We can also change our name. Let the children choose a new name for you and for themselves. Together make new name badges for each child.

Talk about how some changes are very easy: we can change our clothes and even our names without much difficulty. There are other changes that are very difficult, such as changing the way we think and feel and behave. Explain that today's story is about someone who met Jesus and then changed how he thought and felt about other people and how he behaved. He was a greedy and selfish man but with Jesus' help he was able to change.

DELIVER

Deliver the material by telling the story of Zacchaeus. Bring out the aspect of change and Jesus' role in the way Zacchaeus changed. The story could be told using puppets or storytelling or simple drama. Encourage children to reflect on its meaning for us. Jesus can help us change the way we think, feel and behave for the better.

Enact some mini-dramas of times when people behave badly (keep the situations relevant to the children but keep them anonymous). Both children and adults can join in these dramas. Children like to see an adult having a temper tantrum, even if it is only pretend!

Just as Jesus helped Zacchaeus to change, so he can help us to do the same.

Prayer time

Give children the outline of a figure (a child) stuck to a piece of paper or card with a sticky-tape hinge. They can make the figure look like themselves, then lift the figure and write a brief prayer underneath (with an adult acting as a scribe, if necessary). The prayer can be written beforehand and stuck inside if you wish.

Sit in a circle with the figures and place a focus, such as a tray of damp sand and a tealight in a saucer of water, in the middle. Light the candle and say the prayer on the children's cards. Blow out the candle.

Note: Always be very strict about health and safety regulations when using a candle. Place a circle around it (a PE hoop or marker of some sort), which the children may not cross.

If this session were to be planned for 8–10s, a different theme could be selected, such as salvation (rescue). This concept would then drive the exploration of the passage using the 'USED' formula outlined above, with the details of each stage being changed to match the concept.

Planning a youth Bible study on Naboth

UNPACK

Start planning the session by unpacking the story of Naboth from 1 Kings 21. The main concepts in the story are injustice, judgment, and truth and lies.

SELECT

An appropriate single concept to select for a youth group would be that of injustice.

ENGAGE

Engage with the theme by distributing made-up case studies or accounts of unjust situations that have been cut out of newspapers, and ask the group to find what is unjust in each case. Can they cite unjust situations that have been in the news or in the local community?

In groups, improvise dramas about everyday situations of injustice—for example, people being blamed for things they did not do. Using the examples, can the group come up with a definition of justice/injustice? Explain that the story they will be looking at is about injustice.

DELIVER

Deliver the material by reading the story of Naboth. Ask the group to locate the injustice, its cause and results (use highlighters if you are able to photocopy the text).

Discussion starters

- What makes this a story of injustice?
- What does this story tell us about what matters to God and about the nature of God (what he is like)?
- At what point or points could this injustice have been stopped?
- Was Elijah right to condemn Ahab and Jezebel?
- Does this same pattern of behaviour lead to injustice today (in smaller issues as well as murder)?
- What practical things can we do to make the world fairer/more just?

Activities

- As a group, devise a logo or symbol to express the Christian idea of justice (justice reflects a God who is just and fair). What would a symbol of injustice look like?
- Look up material from Christian Solidarity Worldwide (www.csw.org.uk) or Christian Solidarity International (www.csi-int.ch). Make sure the material you use is suitable for your group.

Worship

Place a cross in the centre of the group. The cross is the ultimate symbol of injustice. Encourage people to share their concerns about injustice, big or small, in prayer. The newspaper cuttings and any written prayers can be placed on or around the cross.

Suggested songs

'We'll walk the land' and 'O Lord, the clouds are gathering' would be appropriate songs. Both can be found in *Songs of Fellowship* (Kingsway Music).

CHAPTER 6

A framework for learning

When we do a jigsaw puzzle, we need the picture to help us place the small pieces. In the same way, when we learn, we need the 'big picture' or 'big story' before we are given the detail. If we have too much detail without the overall picture, we can't see the wood for the trees. If we receive lots of unrelated information, our brains don't know how it fits together or to what it relates. Knowledge that is not related to other knowledge tends to be forgotten.

Often we pick up lots of stories and texts from the Bible but do not know how they fit together as part of the 'big story'—the story of God and his relationship with people. We need the big story of the Bible as this is the framework within which we learn about ourselves, God, others and the world. The big story helps us to make sense of our individual stories. Part of discovering meaning and seeing the world differently involves being able to relate the big story to our personal story and situation.

WHAT DOES THIS MEAN IN PRACTICE?

Many of us do not know the overall story of the Bible; we know only disconnected episodes and texts. The big story needs telling in many different ways over a period of time. Whenever appropriate, it is important to say where a particular story or passage fits in with the big story of the Bible.

'Big stories' or 'big pictures' don't have to be spoken; they can be written, drawn or acted. You will find two examples of the big story of the Bible below—a mini-version on page 54 and a longer prose version on page 55. The book *Absolutely Everything* by Terry Clutterham (CPAS/SU) takes 11–14s through the whole story of the Bible and provides a big picture in the form of a board game.

What applies to the whole Bible also applies to smaller sections of it, so, at the beginning of a Bible study series, we need to give the overall 'big picture' of the material we will be covering in the series. It's helpful to have a brief idea of what the passage is about before we start a detailed exploration of it, but we don't need so much detail that curiosity is quenched. For example, 1 Corinthians 15 is a passage about worry and hope. It's about people, like us, who believed in the resurrection but who had questions that needed answering—questions that were unsettling them. In the course of this passage, Paul answers their questions and lays their hope on a firm foundation.

Giving big pictures in this way often supplies a useful mental map or framework. However, it is not appropriate where an element of surprise is needed or if you deliberately want to puzzle people to get them thinking.

The 'big story' in one minute

God made, Adam sinned
Eden lost, world ruined
World flooded, Noah saved
Rainbow signed, promise made

Abraham called, child pledged
Isaac born, Sarah laughed
Hebrews slaved, Moses fled
Egypt plagued, God led

Land conquered, Saul crowned
Goliath slain, David reigned
People lapsed, prophets warned
Nation crushed, temple burned

Daniel prayed, lions starved
Esther dared, people saved
People left, Babylon defeated
Some returned, walls erected

Jesus born, John pointed
People hailed God's anointed
Jesus taught, people saved
Jesus healed, dead raised

Death died, Jesus rose
Spirit came, good news
Word spread, Church grew
Christ returns, all new

© *Margaret Cooling 2004*

The 'big story' in prose

The Bible contains many books but one story. Here is one version of that single story. It can be used as a basis for studies, lessons, sermons and games.

God created the world from nothing, making all that is in it, including us. He made us like himself—creative, powerful and able to love. He trusted his world to us. He formed us to be in relationship with him, but he also gave us free choice. God put Adam and Eve in a delightful place (the garden of Eden) and gave them one command, but they chose to disobey, and evil entered our world. Adam and Eve were excluded from the garden, but not before God had given them a promise: one day evil would be conquered (Genesis 3:15).

Adam and Eve entered a world where they had to struggle for a living—our world. It was a world they had chosen, a world where they set the agenda, for they had chosen freedom without obedience to God. However you understand this story, it reflects the human condition. We are free to make choices; we often choose wrong. Life is a struggle.

God did not abandon his relationship with humanity. He continued to speak to people, but often they chose to ignore him and many chose evil. The world became a place full of violent people, though Noah was an exception. God decided to start again, and a flood covered the earth, but Noah, his family and the animals were saved.

However you understand this story, it's the story of a second chance and God's determination not to give up on humanity but to try another way. God made a covenant—an agreement—with Noah and promised never again to destroy the earth. He gave the rainbow as a sign of this promise (Genesis 9:12–17).

God's new way was to work through a particular people, a people that did not yet exist. First God chose Abraham and called him to leave his home for a new land. Then God entered into another covenant, promising Abraham land and descendants (Genesis 12:1–3). Through Abraham and Sarah, God created a people—Isaac, Jacob, Joseph and his brothers, the founders of the twelve tribes that would eventually form a nation. God wanted to bring this nation into a close relationship with himself and use them as a beacon to show others what a relationship with God could be like. That way, everyone on earth could be brought into a relationship with him (Genesis 12:3).

God continued his relationship with the descendants of Abraham and Sarah, welding them into a people. They were imperfect, but God did not give up. To Jacob and his family he renewed his promise. He was their God, they were his people, and all people would be blessed through them (Genesis 28:14).

The people moved to Egypt, under Joseph's rule. God's promise to Abraham came true: the people grew in number. In fear of this growing nation, the Egyptian Pharaoh made them slaves, but God heard their cries. Through Moses, God led the people out of Egypt and across the desert to the promised land.

On the way across the desert, the people camped at Sinai, the holy mountain. There God's presence was experienced and he once again entered into a covenant with his people (Exodus 19:5–7). He was their God, they were his people, and he would bring them to the promised land. He gave them laws to live by— laws that would show the rest of the world what it was like to live as God's people. He would be with them, and his presence was expressed in the tabernacle, the worship tent that travelled with them.

In the power of God and with Joshua as leader, the people entered the land and settled there. God had kept his side of the covenant: the promise of land had come true. Once in the land, they renewed their covenant with God. They would live as God's people and accept his rule as king. At this time, God was their king and no other; he spoke to them through judges such as Gideon, Deborah and Samson. The people swung between faith and idolatry. They were stubborn and disobedient, but they were God's people and he did not disown them.

The people demanded a king and God gave them kings—Saul, David and Solomon. All were talented and all flawed. With David, God entered a further covenant: one day, a descendant of David would be a great king, a special king sent by God (2 Samuel 7:1–16). In the temple at Jerusalem God also demonstrated his presence in a special way. He was there with them, their God.

Still the people wavered between God and idolatry. After Solomon, the kingdom split into two—the northern kingdom (Israel) and the southern kingdom (Judah). Both kingdoms drifted into worship of other gods, but prophets such as Amos, Hosea, Isaiah, Jeremiah and Micah called them back to the true God. The prophets looked forward to a time when the great king would come (Isaiah 11:1–9), when there would be a new covenant between God and his people, a covenant written on the heart (Jeremiah 31:31–34).

The northern kingdom was invaded by the Assyrians. The southern kingdom was invaded by the Babylonians and her people went into exile—but God was found in Babylon also. He was the God of everywhere; they were still his people. In exile, faith still flourished in people such as Ezekiel, Daniel and Nehemiah. Ezekiel preached God's message of hope that one day Israel would be revived by God's Spirit (Ezekiel 37:1–14).

After many years in exile, the people went home, but only a remnant of the many that had gone away. Under Nehemiah they rebuilt the city of Jerusalem and the temple, though they were shadows of their former selves. Through the priests and prophets such as Ezra, Haggai and Zechariah, God continued to call the people to himself. Some responded, others ignored him. Still the hope lived on, sown by the prophets: one day God would send a special king, the Messiah (Micah 5:2–4).

Not all the people returned; some continued to live faithfully in other places. Esther saved her people in Persia. Then came the dark days between the Old and the New Testaments, when Greek rule and Greek gods were followed by Roman rule and Roman gods (with a brief spell of independence in between). Some of God's people resisted pagan culture, while others compromised. Under pagan rulers they longed for the day when the king promised by God would come.

Finally, God stopped speaking through his prophets and came to live among his people in person. God the Son arrived as a baby in Bethlehem: the king was among us. He not only spoke of the relationship with God; he lived it. People saw the character of God when he touched lepers, comforted those who were sad and welcomed those on the outside of society. They heard God speaking to them when Jesus spoke of God using the language of ordinary things—bread and lamps, wayward sons and kind strangers. They felt the power of God when Jesus healed those who were sick and raised those who had died.

The kingdom of God arrived with Jesus (Mark 1:15). The one spoken of by the prophets had arrived. But he was an unusual king, a king who preached love and trod the path of suffering. He called people to join the kingdom by following the king and living in this world according to the values of the kingdom (Matthew 5—7). In his kingdom everything is topsy-turvy: the first are last and the last first; the weak are strong; love rules and might is not always right.

In Jesus' parables, people learnt of the nature of the kingdom. The kingdom does not come all at once, but grows slowly like a seed. Its future is certain: one day it will be so large that no one will ignore it. The kingdom Jesus spoke of was of such worth that you risked all to possess it. It is both 'already' and 'not yet' (Luke 17:21).

Many joined Jesus; others opposed him. His power challenged theirs. It became a battle that ended on a cross. He took everything they threw at him, including death, and came out loving and living. He took their sins, our sins, and covered them with his blood. Sin and death did not have the last word, for he conquered death through resurrection. The major and deciding battle was over. The power of evil that had marred the relationship with God for so long was broken. It was the beginning of a new relationship —the new covenant spoken of by the prophets.

Jesus returned to heaven and left his followers to pass on the good news of a new relationship with God (Acts 1:1–11). His followers did not work alone, for God came to them in the person of the Holy Spirit to comfort and strengthen them, to inspire and to teach them. The Holy Spirit lived within them, bringing them into the close relationship that they were originally made for. The kingdom spread as more and more people acknowledged the king. Small communities were set up—the very first house churches. Paul and others worked among them, hammering out how to live as a citizen of God's kingdom in this world, looking back to Christ's first coming and forward to when he will return again (1 Thessalonians 5:1–11).

The battle with evil still goes on, for evil is still present in our world, but the outcome of the battle is sure. One day evil will be finished for good, when the king, Jesus, returns (1 Corinthians 15:54–55).

So the message spread and has now been passed to us. We live in the time between Jesus' first coming and his second. We live in the kingdom, but the kingdom is not fully come yet. We try to live by the kingdom values, but we do so in an imperfect world (Philippians 2:14–15). One day, all will be different. Jesus will come again, this time as judge and king. Those who have chosen a relationship with God in this life will continue that relationship, for that is the essence of heaven—being with God for ever. Those who have rejected a relationship with God in this life will have that choice confirmed and continue without God, for that is the essence of hell—the place where God cannot be found.*

The kingdom of God will be established. All war and wrong will end; all suffering and pain will cease. There will be a new heaven and earth, a new Jerusalem, and God will dwell among his people (Revelation 21:1–4). But for now, we are called to live out a relationship with God in the in-between times—until Christ returns.

* Christians differ in the way they interpret heaven and hell.

CHAPTER 7

Pattern and order make learning easier

Our brains search for pattern and meaning, so it helps us to learn if information is ordered rather than jumbled up with no structure. The difference between ordered learning and unstructured learning is like the difference between a jumble sale and a charity shop. In jumble sales, everything is piled up together and we have to rummage to find what we want. In a charity shop, items are sorted into different categories.

This does not mean always having things in a logical sequence; our brains don't always function like that. The brain can learn in many different ways and we can order material in different ways—for example, around a series of metaphors or around the senses.

Think of a number plate or telephone number that you find easy to remember. Why is it easy? One way of remembering numbers or letters is to form sound or visual patterns, or to make meaningful words or sentences. In the case of the number plate FL51 VFW, we might make a sentence: 'a flight lieutenant (aged 51) has a very funny walk'.

If we make a sentence or a pattern of something we want to remember, instead of storing individual numbers and letters our brain stores the information as one single piece (one sentence or pattern). It's like the difference between trying to carry lots of separate items in our arms and putting them into a carrier bag or tying them as a bundle.

The amount we can learn increases if information is sorted into 'bundles' that make sense rather than lots of isolated facts that we have to learn separately. We often need help seeing the patterns in things and in creating the bundles.

WHAT DOES THIS MEAN IN PRACTICE?

We need to group similar or related ideas together to form a 'bundle' of related things. We have lots of unrelated ideas in our heads. We don't always link Easter to the funeral service, John 11:25 and daily life. We need to show how a text links with worship, festivals and ethics, so that these parts of our faith are not divided.

For example, we could link Christmas (celebrating the coming of God the Son) with:

- the nativity crib (born into poverty, one of us)
- the concept of incarnation (God's Son experiencing human life)
- the title 'Immanuel' (God with us)
- the ups and downs of daily life (knowing that Jesus shared them)
- prayer (God understands: he knows what we go through)
- worship (carols such as 'See amid the winter's snow')

We should organize material giving clear headings and subheadings. We can make lists of ideas that belong together, and use bullet points, numbers or a series of images as appropriate. Structuring material in this way helps to reveal the patterns in a text. Keep making patterns and bundling similar things together, but make the links meaningful. Do not connect ideas by trivial similarities such as 'a connection with water', but link them theologically.

- *A group linked by theological themes:* Jacob and Esau (Genesis 33:1–4), the parable of the prodigal son (Luke 15:11–32) and the parable of the unforgiving debtor (Matthew 18:21–35) are all linked by the theme of forgiveness. This is an appropriate 'bundle'.
- *A group linked by colour:* Joseph and his brothers (Genesis 37:1–4), Noah and the rainbow (Genesis 9:9–17) and the heavenly city (Revelation 21:15–21) are all linked by colour, but their theological themes are very different. This would not be an appropriate 'bundle'.

Avoid completely unstructured information. We need to organize material to reveal the pattern that is present in the text but is not always obvious. Sermons, sessions and studies need a clear structure: a sermon that wanders all over the place will be difficult to remember. This does not mean that we have to use a standard three-point sermon; there are lots of different ways of structuring material. For example, we can structure material around:

- a series of important images in the text
- the changing relationships revealed in the text
- patterns of behaviour
- the logical development of an idea

Structuring material can help us to learn, but too much structure can stifle us. We have the ability to process information that is coming to us in different ways—for example, through logical sequence and through a series of images or pictures. If we structure material too tightly, we may fail to use this ability.

Below is an example of a Bible study structured around the theme of guidance. Initially the passage is ordered through the senses, then through actions and words and finally through prayer and worship. Different types of connections are made.

A Bible study on Genesis 24

This sample study explores a key issue in the story of Rebekah and the servant and applies it to everyday life.

Key issue

How does God guide?

Objective

To explore the story of Rebekah and the servant and what we can learn from it concerning guidance.

Getting to know the Bible passage

Read Genesis 24. This can be read as a dramatized reading as there is a lot of dialogue.

Take a 'senses walk' through this passage with the servant. What did he see, taste, smell, touch and hear? Try to enter into his experiences.

Exploring the ideas in the passage

Choose one or more of the following points:

- How does the servant seek God's guidance? Trace his actions and words and create a diagram or plan of his behaviour.
- The servant devised a test. Was it an appropriate test? What would an inappropriate test have been?

- How many times are prayer and worship mentioned? When do they happen in this passage and at what point in the process? What does this tell us about guidance?
- What part did the long journey of the servant have to play in God's guidance?

Application

It has been said that God is more interested in relationships than geography. In other words, when we think of guidance, we spend a lot of time worrying about being in the right place at the right time, but God is more interested in the type of person we are. As a result he often takes us through a long process that changes us when he guides us. Has this been true to your experience?

- Identify times when the process of seeking God's will has brought you closer to God.
- Think about whether the process of seeking guidance has taught you more about yourself and God.

Go back to the objective: what have we discovered about guidance from this passage?

Prayer and worship

People might like to share issues for prayer and spend time thanking God for guidance or asking him for guidance.

There are many images used to describe guidance. As a group, express your own ideas prayerfully by using images. For example:

- Guidance is like holding hands with God in the dark.
- Guidance is like gently pushing open doors.
- Guidance is like following a distant light.

Reflection

Often we see guidance as a puzzle to be solved, a hurdle to be climbed over, or a guessing game with the Almighty ('God has a plan for my life and I've got to find it out').

It may help us to think of guidance as a present to be unwrapped. As we take off the layers of paper, we discover God's will. Often there are many layers. Guidance is an 'unfolding' process that we enter into *with* God.

Close your eyes and imagine a present covered with many layers of wrapping paper. Some layers you have already unwrapped, but there are many still to come. It is a mistake to think that we ever finish unwrapping God's parcel of life. There is always more to discover. His plans for our lives do not recognize retirement age!

CHAPTER 8

Making connections helps learning

The brain is full of cells that are made to connect with each other. Learning happens when a connection is made. Each brain cell can make numerous connections. There are probably more possible connections within the brain than there are atoms in the universe.

The brain likes to connect things: it connects new knowledge with what we already know; it connects knowledge with experience and one part of life with another. We are not always aware of these connections happening, for the brain starts working long before we are aware of it and it goes on making connections long after we have stopped consciously thinking about a question.

WHAT DOES THIS MEAN IN PRACTICE?

Cash in on the brain's ability to make connections without your being aware of it. When preparing a sermon, talk or study, we can read the Bible passage long before we need it and just let the reading 'brew'. Our brain will quietly get on with making connections and we may find ideas just popping into our mind. Sometimes this happens when we are not consciously thinking about a subject, when we're relaxed. The Holy Spirit can work through our minds in this way, so sometimes we just need time and space to listen to what the Holy Spirit is saying.

Our brain's ability to connect means that we should connect what we are currently learning with what has gone before. Teaching and preaching needs to connect to previous teaching or sermons (if part of a series) and with what will come next. We need to remember to connect one part of the Bible with another to fit in with the 'big story'.

We can start a Bible study by asking what is already known about a subject and build from there. By doing this we are using pathways (connections) that already exist in the brain. It's like adding more knowledge to an existing file rather than creating lots of new files. This process also involves everyone in learning and gives us confidence. We are not blank slates; we have something to contribute.

Jesus made connections for people. He connected his teaching to the experience of his hearers as well as connecting it to the Hebrew scriptures. We too need to connect the Bible with experience, but this is not a case of making a token reference to everyday life: it is about making sure that we engage people in order to make teaching relevant.

Engaging is all about making a connection that helps us recall the thoughts and feelings that go with an experience. Just as gears have to engage to create movement, so references to everyday life have to 'move' us. An allusion that does not engage can be like a train going through the station and not stopping to pick us up. Examples of connecting with everyday life can be found in the *Connect* series of studies (produced by Damaris), which use references to TV shows, films and music. Details can be found by visiting their websites: www.damaris.org or www.connectbiblestudies.com.

In the examples that follow, two connections are demonstrated. In the first, *More Bean than Bond*, a fairly brief allusion is made, as the subject is not a difficult one. In the second, *Access Denied*, time is taken to help people recall an experience, as it is a very difficult topic.

'More Bean than Bond': a sermon illustration

When someone mentions the words 'James Bond', one of three people comes to mind. Which one of these three you think of depends largely on your age. The three people are Sean Connery, Roger Moore and Pierce Brosnan.

These three actors, in depicting James Bond, have produced an image of the spy that is suave, smooth and professional. Forget all those images when looking at the biblical spies who are recorded in Joshua 2. These spies are more Mr Bean than James Bond. Let's have a look at the story...

Bible passage

Read Joshua 2.

'Access denied': a reading with a mime

This mime can be used to introduce the subject of judgment—not a popular subject in our culture. In order to connect with people, a cashpoint scenario is used—something that many adults have experienced. A narrator reads the script while one person mimes trying to get money from a cashpoint. The actions, expressions and gestures can be deduced from the script. A group of people mime being the queue that slowly builds up as the script progresses. People can join and leave the queue. The words in bold capitals can appear on an OHP or PowerPoint, or can be read out. The opening only of the sermon is included, so that it can be seen how the mime and the sermon are linked.

Note: the mime is performed facing the congregation.

Bible passage

Matthew 7:15–23

Access denied

You stand at the cash machine.

PLEASE INSERT YOUR CARD
…says the screen.

You insert your card.

PLEASE ENTER YOUR PERSONAL NUMBER

...says the screen.

You lift your hand,
it hovers over the keypad,
you dither for a second,
and then it happens—
you forget your PIN number!
You urgently need the money.
You must try to remember.
You know the number is in your head—somewhere.
It lurks just out of reach, winking at you,
teasing, tantalizing.
For a moment you nearly have it,
but just when you are about to remember—
it slips beyond your grasp.
You can almost hear it laughing
as it drifts away into the depths of your mind.
You try to keep calm. You can do this.
You know that if you don't think about it
the number may just pop into your head.
You try to think of nothing—
nothing happens.
In desperation you type a number.

INCORRECT NUMBER

...comes up on the screen.

You get flustered.
You can feel the queue behind you getting impatient.
You look round and shrug apologetically:
no, you are not a thief with a stolen bank card;
you just can't remember your PIN number.
One more mistake and the machine keeps your card.
You make a decision.

Withdrawing the card, you decide to go to a shop
and buy something you don't want.
That way you can get 'cashback'.
At least they won't ask you for a number!

Opening of sermon on judgment

We live in a society that is full of numbers, codes and passwords. Combinations of letters and numbers give us access to money, services and computer games. Without those PIN numbers, postcodes and computer passwords, the money stays in the bank, the letters go astray, services stay unused and you can't move levels in the game. Without our passwords, we are locked out of society.

What we see in Matthew 7:21–23 is similar to the cashpoint scenario but in this case the scene is the last judgment and it is access to heaven that is denied. The wrong password is used.

'Lord, Lord,' says the speaker. 'We preached in your name, and in your name we forced out demons and performed many miracles.'

'I will have nothing to do with you,' says Jesus.

At the last judgment we will not be asked to:

• Enter a four-digit number
• Type in a password
• Or fill in a form in block capitals

First of all, it will be a personal encounter, not one with a machine. The speaker in our reading comes face to face with Jesus...

CHAPTER 9

Images make connections and help us to learn

Not all the language of the Bible is literal. Non-literal language includes things such as parables, word pictures (images) and metaphors. Word images help us to think; they are not verbal decoration. They create pictures in our minds. If I talk about God as a potter (Jeremiah 18:1–6), I can picture a potter's workshop and the activity involved. If I am just asked to think of God as powerful and creative, that can be a bit more difficult.

Many metaphors connect thinking and feeling, which is probably why the Psalms are so popular.

Jesus used both similes and metaphors. When he said he was *like* a hen who would gather her chicks (Luke 13:34 and Matthew 23:37), he was using a simile, but when he said, 'I *am* the light of the world' (John 8:12), he was using a metaphor (see page 88). Jesus also used many parables. The Psalms and prophetic books are packed full of similes and metaphors, and Nathan used a parable to trap King David (2 Samuel 12:1–9).

Metaphors and similes only illustrate one aspect of an idea; they should not be pushed too far. When we call Jesus 'the good shepherd', we do not mean that he was dirty and poor, as some hired shepherds were. The emphasis is rather on the shepherd as caring and protective. Metaphors have to be taken in context. We need many word images to handle ideas. For example, the Bible uses many images of God—father, potter, judge, shepherd and mother. No one image is completely adequate.

WHAT DOES THIS MEAN IN PRACTICE?

In the church we have to be careful about the word images we use. Using images does not mean using flowery language; it does mean taking time to find the right word picture. When introducing an idea, find helpful images. For example, faith could be described as holding hands with someone you trust as you walk in the dark.

When talking about God, we need to use multiple images. The word 'father' may have different connotations for different people. Someone who had a bad experience of a father may have negative feelings about the word. This is not necessarily a problem, as sometimes those who have had a negative experience develop a very strong sense of what an ideal father should be like. If the damage is too deep, however, alternative metaphors have to be used.

When undertaking preparation, look closely at the text for the images it provides: they may be a way into the subject. The metaphors and similes we use not only enable us to think, but they can also alter the *way* we think. For this reason, we have to be careful in our choice of images. For example, if we call the Bible a 'manual for life', we set up expectations that may not be realistic. Most manuals are specific to a particular model of car or washing machine, but the Bible is not that precise.

Creative prayer activities
using metaphors and images

The prayer and reflection ideas below are for a variety of contexts—church, youth group, Sunday club, housegroups and so on. Select from the ideas as appropriate. The metaphors of the Bible are a rich source of ideas for prayer. Alongside these, we can also create our own metaphors and images.

1. Develop James' image of the small spark (James 3:5). Light a long match and let it burn. Use it to think about the destructive power of words—for example, lying, criticism and gossip. Have damp sand nearby to dispense safely with the spent match.

2. Develop Haggai's image of the bag full of holes (Haggai 1:6) by cutting holes in a carrier bag and pouring some uncooked rice into it (put a tray underneath). Use this as a way of exploring priorities and the danger of putting material things before God.

3. Use a rucksack as an image of the burden of guilt. One person can bring a rucksack to the altar while appropriate prayers of forgiveness are said. Forgiveness is the lifting of the burden (Psalm 38:4).

4. Draw the bars of a prison on acetate. In the bars write some of the things that 'imprison' us—selfishness, anger, pride and so on (Romans 7:15–16).

5. Display a large rock as a way of thinking about God. People should be able to touch it. Display appropriate texts around it—for example, Psalm 18:2, 31; Isaiah 26:4; 32:1–2.

6. A fence or wall can be an image of prayer. Use some plastic garden trellis stretched between two posts. Prayers can be written on strips of paper and woven through the trellis to make a 'fence' of prayer. Alternatively, this could be a 'wall' of praise, thanks or intercession.

7. Place a tray of sand on a table. Trace the word 'sin' in the sand with your finger, then brush it smooth as an image of forgiveness. Leave the tray in the church for people to write and smooth privately during the week.

8. Ask people to hold their right hand in their left hand and grip firmly. Use this as an image of holding on to God and being held: it's a two-way process.

9. Display pictures of weapons and garden implements, along with the words of Isaiah 2:4. Add names of countries that need our prayers for peace, or display suitable stories from the newspapers.

10. Over and over again the Bible talks of God as a refuge—for example, in Psalms 5:11; 7:1; 14:6; 46:1. Remind people of the old custom of taking refuge (sanctuary) at the altar. Invite them to come up during the prayers and kneel at the altar to pray, as a reminder that in God we take refuge.

11. Use a helium balloon as an image of prayers going to God. You can write appropriate words (such as 'sorry') on pieces of paper and attach them to the balloon.

12. A blot is a useful image for thinking about forgiveness. Make a blot with a thick felt-tipped pen on the OHP or flipchart. Then make the blot into a beautiful pattern. Use it to focus prayer on the way in which mistakes can be creative if handled with forgiveness. We can learn from them.

13. Use the image of a clock for prayers of confession. We all have times when we wish we could 'turn the clock back'. We may not be able to do this literally, but God provides forgiveness that enables us to start again.

14. Use Amos' measuring line (Amos 7:7–8) to help you think about coming up to God's standards. Bring in a plumbline and use it as a focus for prayer.

15. Use a piece of broken pottery as an image of feeling broken (Psalm 31:12) and think about the healing role of the Holy Spirit.

16. Using a bucket of water and a dropper, let the drops splash into the bucket from a reasonable height to create a sound. Read Isaiah 40:15, and use it to reflect on the power of God and his *ultimate* control.

17. Place hard and soft objects, such as playdough, Blu-Tack, stones and bricks, on a table. (Make sure they are all safe for the age group you are working with.) Use them for thinking about our ability to change. Sometimes we see ourselves as 'set' (like a stone)—too hard to change. God sees us more like clay (playdough). He can change us (Isaiah 64:8).

18. Use a short clip from a courtroom drama. The Holy Spirit is sometimes called the defender or advocate (1 John 2:1, NIV). With God, it is like having our own defence lawyer. He is on our side.

19. Another way of describing the Holy Spirit is as the 'helper' (John 14:16–18), translated 'comforter' in the Authorized Version. Use children's comfort rags, soft toys and images of parents comforting sad children, to communicate this aspect of the Holy Spirit.

20. Take a candle and snuff it out. Read Isaiah 42:3 (NIV). Demonstrate trying to get a smouldering candle to light. Take two stalks: break one and stake the other. This is how Jesus works with us: he fans the dying flame and does not break the bent stalk. He is a patient, gentle Christ.

How we learn best

CHAPTER 10

We learn best when we use information and engage with it

We learn best when we 'do something' with information—when we use it, when it ceases to be a passive experience and we actively engage with the text. We process food when we take it in, convert it to energy and use it to live. We need to do the same with what we learn. Too often we get regurgitation. Regurgitation is what happens after a dodgy meal: it comes back in more or less the same form as it went down. Information is often regurgitated: we can repeat the words in more or less the same form as they were given, but we can't use them.

One way of learning is to pay conscious attention and turn the learning process from a passive to an active one. This does not mean that we cannot learn unless we pay attention: our brains take in huge amounts without our being aware of it. Paying conscious attention, however, can provide a more effective and lasting way of learning.

WHAT DOES THIS MEAN IN PRACTICE?

Studying the Bible certainly should not be a passive experience. God speaks through the text. The Holy Spirit is active in making the truth of the text live (John 14:26). It is a living word, so we need to interact with it. Part of this process is to ask ourselves a series of questions as we read.

- What does this teach me about myself, others and God?
- Does this affect how I think, feel or act, or all three?
- Does this passage correct, teach or comfort?

Think about the Sunday club. The children may be able to repeat the story of David and Goliath, but can they use it in their lives? We may be able to repeat various texts and beliefs, but have they become part of us? It is important for our lives as Christians that scripture does become part of us.

There is a moment in learning when a 'light' comes on. We might have heard something dozens of times from the pulpit and read it in our Bibles many times. Then suddenly one day we understand. It is the 'Ah, I've got it' feeling. This is, of course, the work of the Holy Spirit. But we can work with the Spirit, removing some of the obstacles in the way of such moments. One way to do this is to change a text or story we are studying into a different form. When we try to express what we think and feel in a different form, we often progress in our own understanding. It is not a case of waiting until we have fully understood before expressing what we understand. Often the understanding comes as part of the process.

Different approaches to a text or story, which can enable obstacles to be removed, include:

- A drama, sketch or role-play
- A diagram
- A question
- A banner
- A video/DVD or book cover
- A summary (for oneself or others)
- A symbol
- A presentation (spoken, or using PowerPoint and so on)
- A gesture
- An activity
- A CD cover
- A ritual that other people can join in

- A form of worship
- A poem
- A song lyric
- Key words on a Post-it note
- A dance
- A prayer
- A metaphor or simile
- A list
- An image—painted, drawn, photographed, described, or imagined

Activities that use information

Select from the suggestions below, according to age group and situation.

CREATING A CD COVER

Imagine that a biblical text has been used as the basis for a song and turned into a CD. Design a CD cover and give the song a title in order to express your understanding of the text.

CREATING LYRICS FROM A TEXT

Some people can express their understanding of a text by creating lyrics or putting new words to well-known tunes.

CREATING WORD IMAGES FROM A TEXT

We can create word images and metaphors to express what we have learned. For example, from Psalm 62, God could be likened to a mountain hut that you find in a blizzard—a place where you can rest in safety.

Creating ritual from a text

A ritual or a reflection that expresses the meaning of a text can be created. For example, for the account of the ascension (Acts 1:1–11), use a large outline of the Jerusalem cross. People can add descriptions of situations around the world where the gospel message of peace and love still needs to be heard. People can come up and add words or pictures to the cross.

The four arms of this cross symbolize the four points of the compass.

Creating a drama from a text

A biblical text can be turned into a drama. For example, Philippians 2:6–11 is shown below as a drama called 'Up and down the ladder'.

You will need:
- Four steps (must be safe and not too high: use stage blocks)
- A briefcase
- A wallet
- A smart jacket and tie
- A casual jacket
- A doll wrapped as the infant Jesus

Cast: Two people (A and B)

Place the props in the correct order on the steps (see script), where they will not be trodden on. Place the baby doll on the floor at the base of the steps.

Note: All items should be dropped to the floor on the congregation's side of the steps.

'A' enters wearing a school shirt/blouse and tie, and stands at the bottom of the first step.

B Well done *(uses A's name)*! Your exam results were really good. I hope you enjoy university.

A takes one step up, removes school tie, drops it to the floor and puts on the casual jacket.

B Well done again, you've got your degree now!

A takes another step up, removes the casual jacket, drops it to the floor and puts on the smart jacket and tie.

B So it's the world of work now. They were really impressed at your interview!

A takes another step and picks up the briefcase.

B Head of your department already! I can't say I'm surprised.

A takes the final step, picks up the wallet and places it in the pocket of the jacket, and then stands still. The briefcase should be held in the hand facing the congregation.

Silence for 5 seconds.

B Although Jesus was by nature God, he did not grasp at being equal with God.

A drops the wallet to the floor, turns and takes a step down.

B Jesus made himself nothing.

A drops the briefcase (loudly) and takes a step down.

B He took the form of a servant.

A removes the jacket, drops it, and takes a step down.

B And was found in human likeness.

A removes the tie, drops it and takes a step down.

B In Bethlehem a baby was born. God had become one of us— Immanuel.

A picks up the baby and cradles it as the final sentence is read.

Note: You may wish to explain to the congregation that academic qualifications are not being condemned in this drama. There is nothing wrong with any of the things mentioned. What is being emphasized is Christ's willingness to reverse the order.

Ways of actively engaging with a Bible passage

Sometimes, when we read a Bible passage, we have trouble remembering it. This often happens because we are not drawing our conscious attention to it and we see it as a passive experience: we are waiting for something to happen. Try some of the questions and activities below; they all involve paying close attention to the text and being an active partner with God.

SENSES

Imagine entering a scene from the Bible. Work through the senses: what would we see, touch, smell, taste and hear? What are the people saying to each other? What expressions would we see on their faces? How are they behaving? Try this activity using Luke 5:1–11.

NAMES

Where appropriate, replace a character's name with your own name and hear the words being spoken to you. Try this using Luke 10:38–42, taking the part of each sister in turn.

VERBS

Go through the passage and highlight all the verbs. What actions are taking place? Are any patterns emerging? Try this using John 1:35–51.

SPEECH AND THOUGHT

Look for speech and thought. Highlight people's words. Are we told anyone's thoughts in the passage? Can we guess their thoughts? Do the thoughts and speech match, or are people saying one thing and thinking another? Try this using Judges 6:1–24.

FEELINGS

Find all the emotions in a passage and highlight them. Sometimes we will have difficulty with this, as in biblical times people did not emphasize emotions in the same way that we do in our post-Freudian age. We may have to deduce emotions from actions in some passages. Try this using Nehemiah 2:1–10.

IMAGES

Look for images in the passage. Some of them may be startling and will help us to think about God, others, ourselves or the world. Look for:

- *Similes:* Similes compare one thing with another, using the words 'like', 'as' or 'than'.
- *Metaphors:* A metaphor is when one thing is described as another, usually using the verb 'to be' in some form (I am... you are... he is... we/they are...). For example, 'God is my rock' is a metaphor.
- *Implicit metaphors:* With implicit metaphors, the verb 'to be' is not used but one thing is spoken of as another. In Psalm 124:3, for example, it says 'anger flared' (NIV). The use of the word 'flared' creates an implicit metaphor of anger as fire.

Try exploring all these kinds of images using Psalm 124.

PAIRS

Work though the passage and highlight pairs. This works well for some teaching passages. For example:

* Behaviour towards God and behaviour towards others
* Things to admire and things to avoid
* Positives and negatives

Try this using Psalm 1 or 1 Corinthians 13:4–8.

DECISIONS

Find an important decision in a story. Why is it important? What led up to this decision? What happened as a result of it? What influenced the person making the decision? Could a different decision have been made? Would it have changed anything? Does the passage help us with our own decision-making? Try this using Matthew 14:1–12.

PEOPLE

Who are the important people in the story? How do we know they're important? Which character do we identify with? Is there a pattern to this person's behaviour? How easy would it be to live with this person? Would we want to live next door to them? If we asked this character what was wrong, what would they reply? Try this using Jonah 4.

SHIPWRECK

Imagine being shipwrecked with this passage and nothing else to read. How helpful would it be? Try this using Hebrews 4.

EXPLAINING

If we had to give a talk to teenagers, what would we say about the passage? If someone new to the church asked us what the passage meant, what would we say? Try this using John 8:1–11.

ENGAGING WITH PRAYER

How can we use the passage in prayer? Write or say that prayer. What does the passage suggest in terms of different types of prayer, such as praise, thanks, confession, asking for help, praying for others or blessings?

Is there a key word or image from the passage that we can use in prayer—for example, as a repeating phrase? Write the key word on a Post-it note and keep it somewhere visible, such as on the fridge or computer. Try this using Psalm 6.

Other things you might look for in a text are:

• Attitudes and decisions
• Hopes and expectations
• Promises, prophecies and plans
• Commands, laws or instructions
• Beliefs
• Messages and advice
• Judgments
• Fears and concerns

CHAPTER 11

We often learn better in context

Many of us remember where we were on 11 September 2001, or what we were doing when we heard the news that Princess Diana had died, or when President Kennedy was assassinated. The context becomes fixed in our mind. Context is important for learning. This does not mean that we cannot learn out of context, but it does mean that the context in which we learn matters. We can create some memorable learning contexts by:

- Creating a stimulating place to learn (the physical setting)
- Creating a stimulating atmosphere in which to learn (the emotional setting)
- Creating learning contexts with the imagination (imaginary settings such as stories and videos/DVDs, role-plays and case studies)
- Using a variety of learning activities (what goes on in the learning context)

Creating a stimulating place to learn

What's on the walls of the room where learning takes place is important. Use displays, posters, questions for people to puzzle over, images and texts. (This may not be appropriate if the church is being used rather than the church hall.) The layout of the room and how people are grouped also matter. Warmth, comfort and other physical factors all play a part. A bare church hall with people in solid rows, facing straight forward, looking at a stage full of chairs and odd bits of junk, is not an ideal setting for learning. (This does not mean that learning cannot take place there if other factors are right.)

Creating a stimulating atmosphere

This is difficult to describe but easy to recognize when we have experienced it. It's about creating excitement about learning. It includes the way we are spoken to, the appropriate degree of formality or informality of the setting, and the use of music and visuals. Worship can be an important way in which we are prepared for learning, as it creates the atmosphere—the emotional context—in which to learn.

Creating learning contexts with the imagination

The brain's power to use imagination is one of the reasons why story works. The story provides a context for considering ideas. So the story of the prodigal son provides a context for thinking about God's love and forgiveness. Video/DVD, TV and films all deal with ideas and issues within stories and situations rather than abstractly. Soap operas often tackle difficult issues in the course of the storyline.

Using a variety of learning activities

Some learning activities make the general learning situation memorable. This is not a licence for gimmicks, however: the learning activity should be appropriately selected to deliver the material being studied. Describe scenes and people, invent case studies, use role-play and drama, and refer to TV and films.

WHAT DOES THIS MEAN IN PRACTICE?

Our ability to use contexts is one of the reasons why the Bible's stories and parables have such appeal. Most people find them easier to remember than laws or doctrine, so create stories around doctrine, laws and texts, for both children and adults.

In his book *Good Neighbours* (National Society/Church House Publishing), Chris Hudson has written a story in which all of the Ten Commandments are broken. It is a superb way of teaching the commandments. Brian Ogden writes lots of stories for young children, to explain beliefs. For example, in his book *Maximus Mouse* (SU), he has a story for each line of the Lord's Prayer.

Put up displays and posters if that's appropriate for the room. Put up thought bubbles where people can express their ideas or ask questions anonymously. Check the layout of the room where teaching takes place. How can you create an atmosphere that communicates the excitement of learning?

Use activities that create memorable learning contexts. Look at the two activities below. The second creates a context, the first does not:

1. Ask the group, 'What sort of person is Jonah? What issues does the book of Jonah face us with?'

2. Imagine Jonah is sitting next to you in the pub or café. Describe what sort of person he is. Would you sit next to him or avoid him? Why? Imagine you strike up a conversation with him. What would you ask him, having read his story? Place an empty chair to represent Jonah. Give people large Post-it notes on which they can write their questions. The Post-it notes can be placed on the chair and used as a basis for discussion.

Activities that create memorable learning situations

Select, from the following list, activities appropriate for the context and the age group you're working with. They are all designed to create memorable learning contexts, either by creating a setting or making the general learning context stimulating. They are also designed to help people engage with meaning.

THE EDITOR'S OFFICE

Imagine you are in the editor's office; she is putting together a book for a new selection of Bible stories. You have to persuade her to include the story you have been studying. What arguments will you use?

THE TELEPHONE CONVERSATION

Imagine that a character who has just witnessed a biblical event phones a friend. What would she say? What would she have remembered? Why? How would the friend respond? Enact or respond verbally.

IMAGINE A PLAY

If your Bible story were a play or film, would it be a comedy or a tragedy or something else? What advice would you give the actors on playing the lead roles? What are the really important things they need to know in order to understand the story and act their parts?

TPPW (TIME, PERSON, PLACE AND WEATHER)

This technique was created by the poet Russell Hoban. People choose a time and write it down or draw a clock in one corner of a sheet of paper. They then choose a character from the story and draw or write the name of their character in another corner. In the third corner, they draw or write a place where that character could have been at that time. Finally they decide on the weather and draw a weather symbol in the final corner.

Each person puts together their four choices, decides what moment in the story it is, and reflects on what their character would have been thinking or feeling at that moment. It can lead to some people writing poetry or prose or just sharing their ideas with someone else. This technique forces people to look at moments in a story in depth.

An example might be:

- 12 midnight
- Joseph
- Outside stable
- Cold and clear

VIDEO/DVD BACK COVER

Imagine that the Bible story you have been studying has been turned into a video or DVD. Write the information for the back cover. Bear in mind what is significant about the story and the time people have to read the information. Why should people take this video or DVD home and watch it?

KENNINGS

Kennings describe things without naming them. They are a form of poetry used by Native Americans and Vikings. For example, 'word scribbler' could be a kenning for a pen. 'Fire water' is a kenning for whisky. 'World maker' might be a kenning for God. What would a kenning for Jesus be? (Perhaps 'heart healer' or 'cross bearer'.)

Your kennings could be included as part of a prayer.

STORYBAG

Use objects related to a biblical story as a focus or to bring out meaning. For example, place a photograph frame, a sandal and an envelope in a bag. These items can be used for the story of Abraham and Sarah leaving Haran in answer to God's call. What part might the sandal have played in the story? Whose picture do you think was in the photograph frame? The envelope is blank and the letter is missing. Who do you think Sarah would have written to? What do you think she would have said about their new life?

The objects are pulled out of the bag at the appropriate moments in the story.

CHAT SHOW

Ask people to imagine that one of the main characters in the Bible story has been invited on to a chat show. What would they be asked? How would they respond? Enact the chat show, with the group creating the questions to get to the heart of what makes a particular character 'tick', or the significance of an event.

ADVICE COLUMN

Imagine that a character from a story has written in to a magazine advice column, and create a dummy letter. What advice would you give?

Alternatively, you can give people the answer and ask them what the original letter may have said. We often find advice in the Bible (in the New Testament letters, or the book of Proverbs) and have to guess the problem behind it.

STORYBOARD

Create a storyboard to communicate the message of a parable in only five frames. First, study the parable and discuss its meaning. Each frame can contain drawings to show the scene. The action can be described, and any dialogue can be written separately. This could be a group exercise, with one person acting as 'artist' and another as 'scribe'.

Alternatively, create tableaux for each scene and photograph them. When they are developed, add captions. Evaluate each other's storyboards.

picture	*picture*	*picture*	*picture*	*picture*
caption	*caption*	*caption*	*caption*	*caption*

CHAPTER 12

We learn best when we use the whole brain

Our brains are made up of two linked halves—and 'linked' is the important word. Both halves of the brain are involved in almost all of our thinking. For example, both sides can be creative, but in different ways; both deal with language, but in different ways.

It has become popular to think in terms of a rigid division between left-brain function and right-brain function. The left side of the brain has been linked to:

- logical thinking
- thinking in a sequence (one thing after another)
- structured thinking
- analytical thinking
- language
- numbers/maths
- abstract thinking
- activities that need concentrated (focused) attention

The right side of the brain has been linked to:

- patterns, image and pictures
- random thinking
- 'intuitive' thinking
- spatial awareness
- rhythm/tunes

- sideways (lateral) thinking
- thinking about the whole thing
- activities requiring less focused attention

However, no one part of the brain is *totally* responsible for any one type of thinking. There is some difference in function but it is not a rigid divide: it is more a difference in emphasis and processing. The brain is a very complex organ and the parts work together.

WHAT DOES THIS MEAN IN PRACTICE?

We need to engage in a variety of activities that use different types of processing and give us different ways of entering a subject or expressing it. For example:

- Explore the 'fruit of the Spirit' (Galatians 5:22–23) by reading the passage and discussing it. Create role-plays to demonstrate each 'fruit'.
- Describe a scene from a Bible story so that people can visualize it, and then explain or discuss what caused the events.
- Follow up a series of images from a text (in any order), then work through the text in a logical or sequential order.
- Brainstorm ideas about the meaning of love and sort them into different categories.
- Sum up the overall message of a passage, then look at it verse by verse.
- Use a painting to investigate a religious idea and explore the application of that idea in daily life.

Look at the youth group session that follows. Are both types of processing being used?

'Time': a youth group session for 14–18s

This session can be spread over two weeks if time is short.
You will need:

- A selection of clocks
- Paper plates—enough for the group plus at least four extra
- Pens and pencils
- Four pots
- Jelly beans in rainbow colours
- The chimes of Big Ben recorded from the news

Objective

To explore our attitudes to time, and to look at some aspects of time in the Bible and what they have to say to us.

Introduction

Have lots of clocks placed around the room. Have ready the chimes of Big Ben recorded from the news. Share the objective with the group and outline the plan for the evening.

Announce that you are going to confiscate all time. Only you will be in charge of it. For tonight, you are the 'Lord of Time'. They must remove all watches and place them in paper bags with their names on.

Put the watches somewhere safe. If possible, bring a box and make a show of putting a chain and padlock on it, place a bag or cloth over it and seal it so that it can't be tampered with. If possible, remove all clocks. Get people involved with these activities as both participants and witnesses.

Select from the material below according to time available and suitability.

GAME

This is a game against the clock—the rainbow bean relay race.

You will need:

- Four teams with four players in each team
- Four pots
- Four plates
- Jelly beans (each team needs seven beans in the colours of the rainbow)

Note: These figures are calculated on a youth group of 16 people. Adjust the items according to your numbers.

Put seven jelly beans in each pot at one end of the room. There should be one of each colour of the rainbow. Place the plates opposite the pots at the other end of the room. The teams stand by their plates.

On a given signal, the first member of the team runs and picks up a jelly bean, runs back and places it on their plate. The next person does the same until all the beans are on the plate. However, the beans must be picked up and placed on the plate in the order of the colours of the rainbow (do not remind the players of the order). Once the beans have been placed, they cannot be changed unless a member of the team completely reruns that section in reverse (they must pick the bean off the plate, put it back in the pot and so on).

Set a time limit appropriate to the group and let them know how much time they have left at regular intervals.

Link

Make a link between the game and time. In the game, time was short and you needed constant reminders of how fast it was passing. Time is something we need to measure in order to be able to tell how fast or slow it is passing. We might also feel that we have too much or too little of it. We are going to take time tonight to consider 'time'.

EXPLORING THE BIBLE: TIME IS A GIFT OF GOD

Read Genesis 1:14.

God gave us a number of years—a length of time. But if you can't measure it, you don't know how quickly it is passing. How does it feel to be without a watch? Can you tell what the time is, even without one?

Ask people to guess the current time. Give them back their watches and check the time. How close were they?

In the past, the moon, sun and stars helped people to tell the time, and we still base our time-telling on them. If we don't measure time, we cannot plan easily. By giving us the ability to measure time, God gave us responsibility for using it.

How do we spend our time?

Read Psalm 90:12 and Titus 3:14. Having only a set amount of time can help us to use it wisely. Take a small ice-cream (soft-scoop if possible), stand it in a glass on the table, and let it melt while the rest of the session goes on.

It's a case of 'use it or lose it' with both time and ice-cream, but that does not mean using it in any way that just 'fills the time'. God made us with minds, bodies, emotions and spirits. We need to balance the way we use time.

Give everyone a paper plate. Ask people to divide it into quarters, labelled 'Mind', 'Body', 'Spirit', 'Emotions'. Ask them to fill in the different sections. How do they spend their time each day or week? Can they put something in each section? Discuss the sort of things that could go in each quarter. Read Ecclesiastes 3:1–8.

TIME DIFFERS IN QUALITY

All time is not the same time. Time, like chocolate, differs in quality.

Have a 'blind' chocolate tasting session, using cheap and speciality chocolate. Can the group tell the difference? (Make sure no one is diabetic or allergic to chocolate: provide alternatives if necessary.)

Place the following sentences on paper around the room:

- I ran out of time.
- It was the best time of my life.
- I waited a long time.
- The time had come to face facts.

We have one word for chocolate, but it can mean slightly different things. We have one word for time, but it can mean different things. Look at the sentences around the wall. How do they differ? Can the group rephrase each one, keeping the meaning the same but not using the word 'time'?

There are several words for 'time' in the New Testament:

- *Chronos:* 'Chronos' often stands for length of time—short or long—such as Matthew 2:7. Which of the sentences round the walls reflects this idea of time? We tend to think of time in the same way that we think of money. We talk about 'spending' time. We try to cram in as much as possible to get value for money.
- *Kairos:* 'Kairos' is often concerned with the character and significance of time, as in Matthew 26:18.
- *Hora:* 'Hora' is the word for 'hour' and is also used to mean significant time, as in John 13:1.

There are some times that are more important than others. Which of the sentences around the wall reflect significant time? Sometimes we treat all time as the same and forget that, as with chocolate, quality matters.

What are the important times for you? When are the times when quality matters, not quantity? Sometimes we let important moments pass us by and do not recognize them as such.

Summary

If appropriate, share significant times with the group. They may wish to do the same. Ask them, in pairs, to think back over the whole session and sum up what they have learned so far. They then take up their paper plates again. How could they get a better balance in their lives? Is there anything they could add or subtract from their lists to improve the quality and balance of their time?

WORSHIP

Use the following worship songs, or appropriate songs of your own choice. (Both of these songs can be found in *The Source: New Songs*, published by Kevin Mayhew.)

- Come, now is the time to worship
- Now is the time (This love, this hope)

Sit on the floor in a circle. In the centre place a clock or the melted ice-cream. Invite people to share their thoughts on the session, in prayer. People can place their paper plates (face down or up) around the clock and silently pray over their own use of time.

Put up the following prayer on an OHP, or hand out paper copies. One person can read the words shown in italic script, while the others join in with the words in bold.

For the time you have given us Lord,
Thank you.
Thank you for the time you have trusted to us.
Give us wisdom to use it wisely.
Thank you for the important times.
Give us the insight to recognize them.
Thank you, God, for giving us time:
time to relax, time to work,
time for ourselves, time for others,
time for you.
Amen.

Emotions and learning

CHAPTER 13

Using the emotional, unusual, dramatic and exaggerated

The emotional, the unusual, the dramatic and the exaggerated (EUDE) tend to grab our attention and fix knowledge in our minds. Knowledge that is highlighted in this way is more likely to be remembered. We notice contrast, and that contrast is supplied by the EUDE. Think of your TV set: the picture is no good if it is all light or all dark. If everything is bright, we see nothing on the TV. The same is true if everything is dull on the set: it's a matter of contrast.

We need to use the emotional, unusual, dramatic and exaggerated at key points in a talk or session to provide contrast. Beginnings are particularly important: we can use them for things we really want remembered. We don't have to make a session all excitement: people need time for thinking and reflection to provide the contrast.

There are two reasons why we need contrast:

The dullness of everyday life

The million small actions that make up life, and the sheer amount of information that bombards us, build up an invisible film like a blanket of snow that dulls the senses and leaves life muffled. For most of us, life is not a round of constant stimulation. The workaday world can dull our senses in all areas; we can experience it in our spiritual lives as well as our ordinary relationships. The unusual, emotional, exaggerated and the dramatic help us to break through this dullness.

The problem of familiarity

We've heard it all before! The Bible is probably the only book that we keep reading and hearing read from the time we are toddlers through to old age. Most books we take back to the library after we have read them once. Unusual versions of the Bible such as the *Street Bible* by Rob Lacey (Zondervan, 2003) make us look at passages in new ways. The emotional, unusual, dramatic and exaggerated help to jolt us out of the type of familiarity that breeds apathy.

Note: This does not mean that we need constant change—that is unsettling. The unusual ceases to be unusual if change is too frequent. For worship, we often need familiar patterns so that we can relax into it.

WHAT DOES THIS MEAN IN PRACTICE?

Sometimes we read part of the Bible and suddenly realize that we have no idea what we have just read. The same sometimes happens while listening to sermons: we hear the words on the margins of our minds but they do not register for any length of time. The emotional, dramatic, exaggerated and unusual help to stop this happening.

To keep attention, some of the following may help:

- Music and worship help to break through the 'blanket' of emotional dullness for many. A worship time can do this, but music can also be used on its own to create an atmosphere.
- We need to think about how we present material. For example, some of us are comfortable giving a dramatic presentation or reading, while others are not. We don't have to do everything: other people can use their talents to help us vary the way material is presented.

- Pay attention to the emotions. Feelings matter as much as the telling; it's the feelings that make the telling fall into place.
- For many, drama, art, poetry, expressive language and dance have the same effect as music. Explore ways of using these art-forms in your church.
- Occasionally break the normal pattern of things. Even in churches with a strong liturgical tradition, there is room for change (see pages 188–191 for guidelines on change).
- Use exaggeration as part of storytelling, as long as the meaning of the text is not distorted. Bob Hartman is a master storyteller. His children's books include *Storyteller Bible*, *Bible Baddies* and *Angels, Angels All Around* (Lion Hudson).
- Prayer can help break through the barriers, especially if it is multi-sensory (see *Multi-Sensory Prayer* by Sue Wallace, SU).
- Approach texts from unusual angles. Examples of ways of doing this in preaching and teaching can be found on pages 111–115.
- Look for the unusual in a text, and for images that will touch our emotions.

Different angles for story (narrative) texts

Because the Bible is familiar to many—we have heard the stories before—we often need to come at the text from different or unusual angles in order to enable us to see what is actually there. Many of the techniques listed below use the imagination, but that does not mean that we are free to do anything with a text. We have both freedom and restraint in our use of the Bible. We are constrained by what is already there, but the Bible doesn't always give us the details or work out the application. There is room for creative thinking within the framework of the meaning of the overall text.

USING POETRY

Poems can often give us unusual insights, angles and perspectives on a text. Sometimes it is just a phrase that gives us the way in. In her poem 'He passed the test' from *Welcome Intruder* (Feather Books Poetry Series), Grace Westerduin uses the phrase 'trial by hope' as a way of describing Abraham's life. Read the life of Abraham again with this in mind.

INFORMATION

Sometimes, just small pieces of information indicate a different way of approaching things. For example, when preparing a sermon on the resurrection, carry out research into the background of life and death in Roman times. Some of the catacombs (Christian burial places) follow the Appian Way. The Appian Way was the road that led directly to Rome. Down this road the Caesars came in triumph. Immediately, there is a way of looking at Christian belief in Christ's victory over death.

METAPHORS AND WORD PICTURES

Look for metaphors and images within the text, which can provide a way in to understanding it. Metaphors and images also give us new means of thinking about a subject. For example, Psalm 62:3 uses the image of a shaky fence, and many of us have had times when we have felt as fragile as a shaky fence.

IF THIS TEXT WERE MUSIC...

Ask yourself, 'If this text were music, what would it be?' Is it a quiet piece of Mozart (Psalm 23) or some other type of music? We need to bear the overall mood of a text in mind when we preach or teach.

MINOR CHARACTERS

Look for the minor characters in a text—the unimportant people, such as the servants in the story of the wedding at Cana (John 2:1–12). Look at the text through their eyes as spectators. What would they have noticed? What questions would have formed in their minds? Prepare your sermon or talk from their point of view.

MAJOR CHARACTERS

Do the same using a major character. For example, what does the parable of the prodigal son (Luke 15:11–32) look like told from the perspective of the father or the older brother? What insights does this give? Does it raise issues that we have to deal with in our teaching and preaching?

INVISIBLE CHARACTERS

Add characters in order to bring out meaning (make it clear you are inventing new characters). What about the prodigal son's mother? What might have been her feelings and thoughts? Use her as a way of reflecting on the story.

THE OBJECT'S STORY

This is an old tradition that goes back at least to Saxon times. Lines from an ancient poem, 'The Dream of the Rood', are inscribed on the Ruthwell cross in Scotland. It is the cross telling its own story. Take an object that occurs in a story. What could it tell us?

SETTING

If appropriate, change the setting: translate the story into our culture and times. What would Jesus' parable of the lost coin (Luke 15:8–10) be in our culture?

CHARACTER DEVELOPMENT

Look for hints in the text that will enable you to develop a character. Things to look for might be:

- What people say and think
- How they react—emotionally and in action

- How they are described
- How others think about them
- How others relate to them

Look at Jonah. What can be made of his character?

PLOT

It is possible to bring out the plot of a story in order to highlight what is happening to the people in the text, and this helps us to understand their responses. Look for the following:

- Statement of problem or situation to be resolved, or issue
- Build-up
- Climax
- Resolution

Try this using 1 Kings 18:1–2 and 15–46.

MAKING LINKS

Link two stories that share themes, using one to bring insights into the other. For example, in medieval times the crucifixion was linked to the near-sacrifice of Isaac (Genesis 22:1–19). Isaac carried his own wood as Christ carried the cross. In the anguish of Abraham we see something of John 3:16. Try comparing the story of Ruth with the parable of the good Samaritan (Luke 10:25–37).

INSIGHTS FROM ARTISTS

We can look at paintings that reflect a text. What insights into its meaning does the painting convey? These insights can be woven into teaching, a sermon or a reflection. (See the examples on pages 116, 147 and 179.)

TEXT FROM AN ARTIST'S VIEWPOINT

Imagine you are an artist who has been commissioned to paint a picture of the text on which you have to preach or teach. Explore it from an artist's perspective:

- Which moment would you choose, and why? (It's not like a cartoon strip: you can only choose one moment.)
- Who would be in the painting?
- How would they be relating to others?
- What would be the expressions and body language?
- What meaning would you want to get across?
- How would you do this?

Asking ourselves these questions during preparation may release new insights. Alternatively, the artist scenario may become part of the teaching session or sermon, as demonstrated in the next worked example.

The artist's perspective

This example is based on the painting *The Marriage at Cana* by Mattia Preti (circa 1655–1660). This picture can be seen on the National Gallery website: www.nationalgallery.org.uk. Go to 'Collection', then 'Full Collection Index', then search by name.

Mattia stood back, put his head to one side and stared at the blank canvas propped on an easel in the corner of his studio. 'I could,' he thought, 'fill my painting with large jars. I could put them in the foreground to dominate the picture, showing the abundant goodness of a God who gave so much wine, a God who gives us life abundantly.' Mattia shook his head. God had supplied abundant wine at the wedding of Cana but that was not the picture Mattia wanted to paint. He wanted to say something different. But what?

For days Mattia had studied the text. He had looked at the way other artists had portrayed the story, and he had discussed it with his friends. He had prayed. Now he had to produce a painting of his own. Mattia took a step closer to the canvas.

'I could,' he thought, 'put Mary and Jesus at the front of the painting, their eyes locked in trust to show the faith that Mary had in her son, the faith that called forth a miracle.'

Again he shook his head; still he was not satisfied.

Mattia took another step forward and continued to stare at the creamy white canvas. It was that, in the end, that solved his problems—a plain, white cloth. With a few stokes of his brush Mattia painted a table, its end filling the front of the picture, its sides slanting away into the background. A few more strokes of his brush and he covered the table with a plain, white cloth that flowed over its surface and fell to the floor, creating a rectangle of cloth over the end of the table—a canvas within a canvas.

The thoughts came thick and fast: within moments the outlines of servants kneeling on the floor were drawn. Next came the water pots, also on the floor. Sitting at the end of the table were Jesus and the best man. The best man reached down to the servants and in his hand was a single glass of wine against a white cloth.

Mattia stepped back. He had his painting. All the action was taking place on the floor and against the background of that rectangle of cloth, well below the level of the table surface, well below the eye level of the guests. Only two people besides the servants knew what was happening—Jesus and the best man.

If we had been asked to paint a picture of the wedding at Cana, we too might have painted a glass of wine—but we would probably have put it on the table. Mattia Preti shows it being passed, unseen, underneath the edge of the table, across a white cloth. This was Jesus' first miracle. He began as he meant to go on. Jesus did not use his power to draw attention to himself for selfish ends, but at a family wedding he cared enough about an unnamed couple to rescue the situation quietly, and in doing so he spoke volumes about God.

This miracle, like the other miracles in John's Gospel, was a sign that pointed to who Jesus was—the Messiah. But he was a different type of Messiah from the one most people expected. This Messiah had power, but he used it for others. This Messiah had come to free his chosen people and also the rest of the world. This Messiah had come to reveal what God was like, and he started at a country wedding.

Note: This example could be used as the opening of a sermon or talk.

CHAPTER 14

Challenge, pressure and learning

Challenge helps learning; too much stress or pressure for too long a period reduces it. Some stress or pressure stimulates learning for many, but individuals vary in the amount they can cope with. What is mild stress for one is too much for another. Understanding how people react to stress and pressure and how it affects their learning helps us to adapt our teaching.

If we feel threatened, our body goes into survival mode. It becomes difficult to think because resources are switched elsewhere and we revert to certain types of behaviour, none of which is good for learning:

- Flight (avoidance)
- Fight (aggression)
- Flock (gather with like-minded people who think like you: safety in numbers)
- Freeze ('Help! I don't understand': temporary paralysis in thinking)

The following factors help to relieve stress:

- Outlets for frustration
- A sense of control or predictability
- Support from others
- A sense of things improving

WHAT DOES THIS MEAN IN PRACTICE?

Teaching and preaching should challenge, but should not stress or pressurize inappropriately. If we feel threatened, learning can be impaired. For example, guilt often creates stress. There is a place for guilt—it is God's warning system—but such feelings should never be induced without a way out. We should never take the lid off a can of worms unless we can put it back on again. One way of unnecessarily creating guilt is to set up unreal expectations—for example, suggesting that prayer is always easy or that reading the Bible is always exciting. If this is done, the following scenario may happen as the result of the stress caused.

We come from the busyness of work and family life and we expect the words of the Bible to leap off the page and speak to us, for we have been told that reading the Bible is always exciting. We want to feel excited about God's word, but sometimes it just does not happen: we go away disappointed. We go away with information, but it does not live for us.

People react to this experience in several ways:

- Sometimes we blame ourselves. We were told by someone in authority that the Bible is exciting. We believe that the Holy Spirit inspires the Bible, so if it is not exciting there must be something wrong with us.
- Sometimes we blame God. He promised inspiration, his ministers promised excitement, and it did not happen. The result may be a loss of faith.
- Sometimes we lower expectations. We just stop expecting much.
- Sometimes we play a 'game', pretending that it is always exciting to read the Bible. (This can lead to enormous guilt feelings in others or a form of communal 'game-playing'.)

More realistic teaching on using the Bible in our devotional lives, which faces both the difficult times as well as the excitement, could reduce this stress. The Bible is not an airport thriller. We cannot expect *instant* excitement for a small amount of investment of time and effort.

Make sure there are channels for talk and involvement so that people do not have to sit on their frustrations. Celebrate success and growth: too often we only notice what goes wrong. Keep people informed to give a sense of predictability.

We need an environment where it is emotionally safe to learn (p. 32) and where we can support each other. Only in such an environment are we free to take risks in learning and tackle the genuine problems and possibilities of Christian living. The relaxed atmosphere of Alpha courses is an example of this. The church should not be a place where we have to fear put-downs, being laughed at or heresy hunts.

There is evidence of a period of unsettling before we grow in faith. The way faith is held (not necessarily its content) sometimes has to be dismantled and rebuilt in order to move on to maturity. Churches often find this stage difficult to cope with and, as a result, people either get stuck in an immature faith or leave the church altogether.

Asking questions and probing the boundaries is not necessarily a sign of lack of faith; it can be a sign of growth. If we are going through this stage, we need security and encouragement rather than being made to feel that we are failing or 'backsliding'. Such attitudes only increase anxiety. What is needed is a change of attitude and a willingness to talk if need be.

The following sermon could be seen as threatening, as it likens our behaviour towards God to unfeeling teenagers and challenges people to change in the light of God's judgment, but a way out is offered (a sense of things getting better, a hope of change).

A sample sermon on Isaiah 1:10-20

I have with me a box of things that I treasure. *(Show box and items.)* There are pictures done by my children at various times. There are also things they have made for me—a pin-cushion with the pins forming a heart, given by my eldest son; a drawing of the family by our foster-daughter; a brooch given me by my youngest son. I'm normally very unsentimental, but some of the Mothering Sunday gifts I have been given I will keep for good.

There is, of course, the opposite extreme. Sometimes Mothering Sunday is used as an excuse to be sentimental. I would like to read you a few verses from some commercial 'Mothers' Day' cards. *(Read some very sentimental cards.)* Personally this type of card does nothing for me. As a teacher I observed that some of the most badly behaved children made some of the most sentimental cards to give on Mothering Sunday—and I know they gave their mothers a hard time!

I would like to read a reflection. I want you to imagine a mum with teenage children who are very, very badly behaved—an imaginary family. They walk all over her and treat her as a servant. They never appreciate what she does, but once a year they buy her a card and give her flowers.

The card lied.
'The world's best mother,' it said.
She would have settled for 'She tried.'

The flowers were offered.
She took them but she did not want them.

They were part of a tired ritual,
a conspiracy of lies:
they said nice things,
she smiled and looked grateful.
No one was deceived,
but no one wanted to rock the boat.

They were buying her silence
with a sentimental card and cheap flowers.
She longed for the courage to give them back—
to explain that she did not want flowers.
She hated the sugared words of the card,
they made her feel dirty, compromised,
a boxer throwing a fight.
But if she gave them back, they would have to change.
She would have to challenge their behaviour
and she was frightened of losing what little love they gave her.

This was her day,
but all she was offered was a veneer of affection,
soft love, indulgent words.

She wanted to stop the farce,
to break the truce.
She wanted to say, 'Let's get it out in the open, shall we?
You kids treat me like dirt all year,
then buy me flowers and a card on Mother's Day,
and you expect me to be grateful!

'You expect me to be satisfied with the bone of affection you throw me;
the fag end of your love that costs you nothing.
You should be pleased with yourselves.
You have worked out the maximum return
for the minimum amount of effort!

*'Take back your flowers
and your card.
Give them to me next year—
but only after I have seen your love in action.
Only if I see that I matter to you.*

*'And don't send me a card that says, "The Best Mum in the World";
simply write: "We love you and we tried to show it."
Then I will accept your gifts,
I will listen to your words.
I will hug your affection to myself,
knowing that you return my love.'*

*She will not, of course, say any of these things.
She will continue to accept the flowers,
read the card with a weak smile,
nurse the insult of superficial love.*

*Like diplomats of countries on the verge of war
they will play the game,
pretend all is well,
but inside, part of her will die.*

© *Margaret Cooling*

God is both father and mother to us. In this passage from Isaiah, God refuses the gifts his people offer—sacrifices, incense, prayer and offerings (see verses 11–15). These were all part of the ritual of worship. God refuses to hear their prayers (see verse 15) and makes it clear that he does not accept their worship. It is like the mother refusing the cards and the flowers. It was not because sacrifices or any of the other parts of worship were wrong. It was because the worship was not matched by the way in which they lived their lives (see verses 15–16). What Isaiah said of the people of Israel thousands of years ago still applies to us today.

Christianity is a religion about a relationship. It's not primarily about getting the ritual right. It's not about getting the words right. It's about getting the relationship right and then expressing the love experienced in that relationship in worship and in daily life.

The relationship with God (faith) and the practice of that faith in daily life (deeds) cannot be separated. They are two sides of a coin. They are like the lines that make up the letter 'L' of love. It needs both a vertical and a horizontal line to complete the letter. *(Demonstrate on the OHP or flipchart.)* True faith must be practically expressed. Isaiah gives us examples—doing justice, stopping evil, looking after widows, orphans and those in need of help (see verse 17). The Bible constantly repeats this message, such as in the following passages:

The Lord God has told us what is right and what he demands: 'See that justice is done, let mercy be your first concern, and humbly obey your God' (Micah 6:8).

I, the Lord, hate and despise your religious celebrations and your times of worship. I won't accept your offerings or animal sacrifices—not even your very best. No more of your noisy songs! I won't listen when you play your harps. But let justice and fairness flow like a river that never runs dry' (Amos 5:21–24).

In Matthew 21:28–31, the parable of the two sons, Jesus asked which of two sons did the will of the father—the one who said he would work but didn't, or the one who said he wouldn't but changed his mind and actually did the work. Jesus left us in no doubt about his response to the question!

Anyone who doesn't breathe is dead, and faith that doesn't do anything is just as dead! (James 2:26).

We cannot buy God's silence about our behaviour by church attendance, much praying, or reading of the Bible. He will be deaf to our prayers if we are deaf to other people's needs. God is not easily fobbed off. He does not wink at our sins and, unlike the mother in our reflection, he is not afraid of tackling us for fear of losing our love. God is long-suffering but he is nobody's fool. He will not accept worship on Sunday if it does not make a difference to Monday.

Look at Isaiah 1:18–20. This is a call for us to change, and God offers to do the changing in us. The tone then switches, and becomes much softer. 'I, the Lord, invite you to come and talk it over,' God whispers. However, the verbs that follow are very definite:

Your sins are scarlet red, but they will be whiter than snow or wool.'

When we read this passage in the light of Jesus' words in John 3:16–17, we get the full picture:

God loved the people of this world so much that he gave his only Son, so that everyone who has faith in him will have eternal life and never really die. God did not send his Son into the world to condemn its people. He sent him to save them!

God is not some distant judge who points out sin. In Jesus, God was fully human and fully understands our situation.

In the Middle Ages, when God was depicted as judge he was depicted sitting on a rainbow (a symbol of hope), with the sword of justice in one hand and the lily of mercy in the other. Hope and mercy outnumber justice—we get more than we deserve.

The one who outlines the problem provides the solution.

He has done everything necessary to change us—if we let him. *He* has the power to change us—if we let him. *He* is longing to change us—if we let him. There is nothing to stop God changing us—except our unwillingness to be changed.

CHAPTER 15

Emotions and learning are linked

Learning that does not address the emotions and the will, as well as how we think, only does part of the job. Emotions and learning are linked in a number of ways:

- The feelings of the learner (just had a row with boyfriend)
- The feelings of the teacher (had a really good day)
- The feelings they have about each other ('That difficult person'; 'I really like it when Abby leads the housegroup')
- Their feelings about the environment they are in ('The church hall is a mess!')
- Their feelings about what they are learning and teaching ('I can't see the point of this'; 'This is really challenging')

Some of these factors we can do little about; others we can influence. We can create good emotions associated with learning. These increase the output of chemicals that make us feel good: laughing is good for us and we are never too old to be told we are doing well. A sense of belonging, being noticed or having your contribution recognized also help. These are all part of creating a positive atmosphere for learning. Negative emotions, such as fear and feeling ignored, can hinder learning,

We tend to look at new information and filter it for emotional value and relevance. Emotions attached to information make us take notice and help us to remember, for the strength of the output is often related to the strength of the input. For example, talking about accepting God's will and plan for our lives can seem rather 'cold'.

Using the image of burying one set of dreams for the future and embracing God's new future is a warmer image that makes contact with the emotions.

If we feel upset by new information, we will often reject it. We may feel threatened and take a defensive position. Once we have done this, it is difficult to back down. The emotions can hijack thinking in this way and make learning difficult.

WHAT DOES THIS MEAN IN PRACTICE?

We can use humour and praise, for they can be part of creating a positive learning atmosphere. This does not necessarily mean telling jokes (unless they fit naturally) but it does mean finding the natural humour in situations: as Christians we can sometimes get a bit too serious. Noticing what others do well and thanking them is also part of creating a good learning atmosphere. We shouldn't just notice when something goes wrong or doesn't happen.

Acknowledge the role of emotions in learning. We can reason that something is true in sermons and studies, but if we ignore the feelings involved in learning, the information is likely to be forgotten. This does not necessarily mean becoming 'emotional' or sentimental, but it does mean becoming 'real'. When something strikes us as 'real' (reflecting the world and experiences we know) it touches our emotions, we see its significance and we tend to take it to heart and apply it. In some cases, this means accepting vulnerability and sharing appropriate personal experience with each other rather than staying at a distance. It sometimes means acknowledging the gap between what we aspire to and what we actually do.

The emotional side of learning is not an optional extra; it cements knowledge in our minds. Knowing that emotions are powerful in learning means we need to be careful how we use them. It is acceptable to engage the emotions as part of learning, but it is unacceptable to manipulate emotions. We have to ask ourselves some searching questions:

- *Intent:* Am I engaging emotions to learn, or to get people to do what I want or to feel a sense of power?
- *Degree:* How far do I need to engage emotion? Is this 'over the top'?
- *Responsibility:* Can I handle the situation responsibly once people are engaged?

Be aware that some teaching and preaching, by its nature, may challenge our thinking about God, ourselves, other people and the world and result in an emotional reaction. One of the most stressful situations is when someone seems to be undermining our faith, so it is important to warn people if we think that this is likely to happen. We need to acknowledge that some people may feel as if we are being negative although that is not our intention. Explain that you have to go through the process in order to put things on a firmer footing. We might have to ask others to bear with us until we get to the constructive part. Forewarned is, to a certain extent, forearmed.

The sermon in the following worked example picks up on how mind, body and emotions are linked, not only in content but by form. Other examples of addressing emotions as well as mind and action can be found on pages 121 and 172.

A sample sermon on 1 John 3:11-24

This sample sermon, entitled 'The agony uncle', starts with the following one-sided conversation on a mobile phone:

He never did!
You must be joking!
No, of course I won't.
See you tomorrow.
Bye.

Reading the letters of the New Testament is a bit like listening to a one-sided telephone conversation—you have to guess what the other person is saying. This passage of the Bible is taken from a letter. We must never forget this. John was not writing abstract advice; he was answering a practical problem. Someone had asked a question or a series of questions, and we have to work out what the question was from the answer. Maybe it will help to think in terms of an agony aunt or, in this case, an agony uncle.

I have composed a question to an agony aunt that addresses similar issues. Maybe it will help us to understand the situation that John was addressing.

Dear Jane
My boyfriend and I met in quite dramatic circumstances. We were on a sailing holiday and I was accidentally struck on the head. This caused me to fall over the back of the boat. As we were on engine rather than under sail

at the time, the situation was quite dangerous. I could have been injured by the propeller! Dan shouted for them to cut the engine but, instead of waiting, he jumped straight in and pulled me clear. I didn't realize how much he risked to save me until I saw his glove. The fingers of one glove were shredded by the propeller!

Well, we have been together now for about two years. Dan is loving and kind, but it is not exciting any more. How do I know he really loves me? Come to that, how do I know I really love him? I feel guilty even asking this question as he is a really good person.

Yours, Emma

The answer you get to such letters depends on who you write to. Here are some possible replies. The no-nonsense response…

Dear Emma, For heaven's sake, woman, stop whinging! Consider yourself lucky to have such a man. There are thousands of people with much bigger problems than yours, so pull yourself together.

The Mills and Boon response…

Dear Emma, It sounds as if the romance has gone out of your life. You need to put the romance back in. Have you tried a candlelit dinner? How about having a makeover so that you once again attract him in the way you originally did?

The Bridget Jones response…

Dear Emma, I know exactly how you feel. I too have constant agonies over the men in my life. None of them quite live up to my expectations.

P.S. If you don't want Dan, please send his address by
return of post. SAE included.

I'm sure you will agree that none of these responses is adequate.
None of them take the whole person into account. The person to
whom John was writing seems to have expressed similar concerns
about the Christian faith as those expressed by Emma about Dan in
her letter: 'How do I know that God loves me?' (verses 16 and 24);
'How do I know that I love him?' (verses 14 and 17); 'I feel guilty'
(verses 19 and 20).

First of all, John does not go in for the no-nonsense approach and
tell his correspondent to snap out of it. Second, he does not take the
Mills and Boon approach and just address the feelings. Third, he
does not take the Bridget Jones approach and just sympathize.

John is a model of a good agony uncle. His reply takes account of
the whole person.

He takes the questions seriously. Just because there are worse
things happening in the world, it doesn't mean that this type of
question isn't a real concern. Worse things happening in the world
may put some of our questions into perspective, but it does not
mean they have to be ignored.

John responds to the first question: 'How do I know God loves me?'
John points his correspondent to an event, a moment in history—a
date as real as 1066. He points to a moment when God walked this
earth in Palestine (verse 16). He refers us to a moment of time in the
first century when a young man in his early 30s—God's Son—hung
on a cross. It was a moment in the past that, as Christians, we
believe changed the future for ever—an event that expressed God's
love, not in words, not in feelings, but in action.

You cannot measure the inspiration of a symphony or the beauty
of a work of art.

The same principle applies to love. Love cannot be measured in
feet and inches or in centimetres and metres. The breadth of God's
love is measured in the distance between two outstretched arms
upon a cross.

131

John refers us back to that event. Knowing that we are loved by God doesn't depend on feelings: they vary depending on our circumstances and our hormones.

- If I feel confident in God's love—he died and rose for me.
- If I feel doubtful about his love—he died and rose for me
- Nothing changes the fact that he died and rose for me.

John responds to the second question: 'Do I love God?' When John deals with the question 'Do I love God?' he does not recommend navel-gazing. We will not find out if we love God just by thinking about it. We know we love God if we behave in a loving manner. In verses 17 and 24, John talks in terms of obedience: we know we love God by the presence of the Spirit, helping us to obey, helping us to live how God wants.

Our emotions and our thoughts and actions are not always synchronized. Sometimes we are like a film where the sound is not quite in line with the movement of the actor's mouth. If we wonder if we love God, the answer is not just to sit worrying about it. The answer is to act. If we act lovingly and speak lovingly, often the emotions catch up and we feel the love. This is not hypocrisy; it is reality. It is recognizing that our emotions are sometimes wayward and we have to learn to discipline them and bring them in line with our commitment.

John deals with the final issue: 'I feel guilty'. This is partly a personality factor. Some people feel guilty all the time. Some people rarely feel guilt. For those who do experience guilt, John offers a reminder. He does not tell us off for feeling guilty, because the emotion is genuine and it needs dealing with. We need to set our hearts at rest (verses 18–20). When we feel guilty, we need to look back at what Christ has done for us, act in a loving way towards others and always remember that God is greater than any doubts and worries we may have. He can deal with them. God is not threatened by our doubts.

So John's reply deals with the whole person:

- The mind—he refers us to an objective event.
- The body—he gives us something to do.
- The emotions and the spirit—he does not ignore our feelings or the work of the Holy Spirit.

John leaves us able to worship the Lord our God with all our heart, with all our soul and with all our strength.

Note: If desired, the 'letters' can be read by other members of the congregation.

CHAPTER 16

Motivation and purpose are important for learning

Motivation is emotion on the move. If we know why we are doing something, we learn more. We can't notice everything so we filter out information that we do not think is important. One of the things that decides the importance of a piece of information is whether we think or know that it is relevant to our aims in life, our needs and our beliefs. We are not motivated to learn things that we don't think are relevant. Most of us either consciously or unconsciously ask the questions 'What's in it for me?' and 'Is it worth doing?'

A leader may know the purpose of a particular activity but, unless it is made known to everyone, others are left wondering why they are doing it. It is not enough to know that we are studying a certain passage 'in order to be a better Christian': that is so vague that it could apply to any passage. Goals should be specific and achievable. Don't set up failure by making over-ambitious goals.

WHAT DOES THIS MEAN IN PRACTICE?

The Bible is strong on purpose and goals. Paul talks of pressing onwards to the goal. He likens the Christian life to a race and Christians to athletes who train for a purpose (Philippians 3:12–14).

Has your church got a clear sense of mission? Does it know where it is going? A church's overall 'vision' matters, as it gives a sense of purpose and direction. As a congregation, do we know the purpose of Bible studies? Do the youth group know why they are exploring a particular subject? Two basic questions need to be asked:

- Why am I teaching or preaching this?
- Why do we need to know this?

Information for information's sake does not motivate us to learn. We should often work on a 'need to know basis' when selecting information for teaching and preaching. Unnecessary detail can get in the way of understanding. We need to take time to explain the relevance of what we are doing.

Teaching and preaching should match our needs or help us to become aware of our needs. It is also important to have a say in what is taught to us. When we have an investment in something, we are more motivated.

Having a purpose for an activity is not enough; it needs to be a known and achievable purpose. This gives focus to our planning and learning and allows us to assess our effectiveness. If we have a purpose (a goal or objective), we can check to see if we have achieved it. If we fail, we can ask the following questions:

- Was the goal too ambitious?
- Was it taught in a way that could be understood?
- Was it a joint goal: were we all going for it?

State the purpose (objective) at the beginning of a programme. At the end, take time to discuss whether it was achieved. Give people a focus (a purpose) when you ask them to read a passage; give them something to look for. For example, read Genesis 12:10–20 as if you are a reporter for a tabloid newspaper. What would strike you?

A number of other factors affect motivation in the church. Read through the following list and think about your own situation.

- We learn better in a setting that helps us to succeed and gives us confidence. Good learning experiences encourage a 'have a go' attitude.
- Plan activities for early success. If possible, don't do the most difficult bit first.
- If we are noticed, affirmed and encouraged by others, we are more likely to take the risk of trying new things. Being ignored kills motivation.
- Constructive feedback and recognition can help improve our teaching and learning.
- Hope and enthusiasm matter. Apathy and cynicism kill motivation.
- Having the resources to learn helps: provide training, people, space, time and books if necessary.
- Strong personal goals and any internal or external rewards help to motivate us. This might include personal significance or studying for a qualification such as Reader or lay preacher.
- Being able to see progress and success in learning at a personal and church level motivates. Some churches encourage people to keep spiritual journals; others give people a few minutes in the service to share the way in which something they have learned has helped them to progress.

A Bible study on John 1:6-8, 15, 19-28

In this example, the objective is stated in terms of a question that people try to answer at the end of the session.

Objective

By the end of this study, each member of the group should have explored the work of John the Baptist and thought through his or her own ministry. Group members should reflect on their answers to the key question at the end of the session.

Key question: What can we learn about our own work for God from the way John describes his ministry?

OPENING ACTIVITY

Ask each person to state one thing they are and one thing they are not. This is only an icebreaker; it does not have to be profound! For example, 'I am a nurse. I am not David Beckham.'

Explain that we will be looking at John the Baptist's ministry and identity and reflecting on our own Christian ministry. Read the key question. Ask people to bear it in mind in the course of the study.

BIBLE READING

Read John 1:6–8, 15, 19–28.

Background information

Tell the group that, in this passage, John is asked a series of questions about who he is. Each of the people mentioned is important:

- The 'Christ' or the 'Messiah'—the king sent from God.
- 'Elijah'—one of the great Old Testament prophets who would appear before the Messiah came.
- 'The Prophet'—a 'Moses' figure who would repeat the miracles of the exodus (the escape from Egypt).

Getting to know the passage

1. Look at the way John's ministry is summed up positively. Look for all the things that John came to do (take a close look at the verbs describing his work).
2. Now look at what John is not (vv. 8 and 19–21).
3. Why do you think John's ministry is summed up both positively and negatively?
4. Read verse 23. How does John describe himself?
5. What do verses 23–27 tell us about John as a person?

ACTIVITY

Think about your own Christian ministry and your own life. In one sentence sum up positively what you feel your work for God is. For example:

- I feel that my work at the moment is to bring up my family and show the love of God to them.

Sum up your calling negatively. For example:

- I don't feel, at the moment, that my ministry is to wider evangelism.

Share individual responses with the group. If people don't want to share their thoughts, they can just say 'pass'.

Discuss the following questions:

- Is it important to know what our calling is and is not? Why? Why not?
- How can knowing our calling help in saying 'no' to some things and 'yes' to others?
- In what way can it help with guilt feelings about not doing everything?
- In what way can it help us focus on doing something well?
- Does the answer to the question change at different times in our lives? Why? Why not? (People may wish to share examples here.)

Application

Think through one situation where knowing what you are, and what you are not, might be helpful in making decisions. Share these thoughts if appropriate, either with the person next to you or the whole group.

REFLECTION

If you were asked to describe yourself in terms similar to John the Baptist ('someone shouting in the desert'), what phrase would you use? Some examples might be:

- I am a hand reaching out to the lonely.
- I am a voice speaking of God to others.
- I am a shoulder to cry on.
- I am a mind thinking for God.
- I am a worker showing what honesty is.

Many people concentrate on what they are. Sometimes knowing and accepting what we are not is just as helpful. It stops us striving after the unattainable or what is not right for us at a particular time. We need to affirm the gifts and calling we have and be able to accept what we are not. This stops us wasting our energies and giving in to pressure.

Go back to the key question and ask the group to share their thoughts in response to it.

Learning and difference

CHAPTER 17

We learn in different ways

We all learn differently. One of the ways we differ in learning—and it is only one—is the way we use our senses to learn. We take in information through our senses, but people differ in the sense they prefer to use when learning new or difficult material.

THE THREE LEARNING PREFERENCES

We can remember the three learning preferences by using the acronym 'VAK'. VAK is short for:

- Visual (seeing)
- Auditory (hearing)
- Kinaesthetic (doing/feeling)

Visual learners

Approximately 29 per cent of people are visual learners. If we are visual learners, we like to see information in writing or pictures. We visualize scenes so that, even if information arrives in a spoken form, we can still use our ability to 'see' things in our mind's eye.

Auditory learners

Approximately 34 per cent of people are auditory learners. If we are auditory learners, we like to hear information, to discuss and talk to ourselves; we carry out silent conversations or run words through our minds.

Kinaesthetic learners

Approximately 37 per cent of people are kinaesthetic learners. If we are kinaesthetic learners, we enjoy the physical and emotional feelings that go with learning. We like learning by doing. Kinaesthetic learning is not all action, however. We enjoy the feelings that learning brings—the 'tingle factor'—the excitement of grasping something and the struggle to understand.

We should not think of people as just visual, auditory or kinaesthetic learners. We use all three styles of learning, even though we may have an emphasis on or preference for one style.

The Bible is full of examples of different types of learning. The prophets used dramatic actions, such as wearing a yoke or cutting off their hair. They also built up visual pictures in the way they described God, such as that of the shepherd in Psalm 23 and Isaiah 40:11, or of a parent teaching a child to walk in Hosea 11:3. The Psalms and other poetic sections of the Bible use the rhythm and pattern of language. The festivals of the Bible, such as the feasts of Tabernacles and Passover, use participation to reinforce faith: people lived in tents in order to remember the years in the wilderness, and they tasted bitter herbs to remember slavery.

WHAT DOES THIS MEAN IN PRACTICE?

Being aware that we learn in different ways has implications for both teachers and learners. We need to use a range of styles over a period of time, not necessarily all three every time (unless we feel we can do this). We need to take responsibility for our own learning and become more aware of how we learn, helping ourselves by devising ways of learning that suit us.

Visual learners (by eye)

For visual learners, sermons and teaching sessions can be accompanied by written headings on an OHP or PowerPoint or on a printed sheet. Objects and images can be used to illustrate points. Scenes can be visualized and the imagination stimulated.

Auditory learners (by ear)

Sermons and talks can draw on the rhythms, sound and patterns in speech, such as:

- *Alliteration:* using words beginning with the same letter, such as 'sin' and 'salvation' (but don't overdo it).
- *Assonance:* using words that share vowel sounds, such as 'save' and 'stay'.
- *Repetition:* the creation of pattern and rhythm. (The end of the sermon on page 121 uses repetition.)
- *Rhythm:* the pattern of stresses on different words and syllables makes a rhythm. (This technique is used in 'The "big story" in one minute' on page 54.)
- *Letter sounds:* letters and syllables have particular sounds (soft, hard, flowing, staccato) that help to create moods. A soft syllable at the end of a word—for example, 'away'—creates a different feel from a hard sound such as 'depart'. Choose words to fit with the mood of the text.
- *Rhyme:* the last one or two syllables of a word match in sound, such as 'love' and 'dove' or 'battle' and 'rattle'. Half- or near-rhyme can also be used, such as 'burned' and 'warned'. Rhyme can lose its effectiveness with over-use. Rhyme does not have to come at the end of a line; it can come in the middle or beginning.
- *Onomatopoeia:* words that sound like their meaning, for example, 'gargle' and 'ooze'.

Kinaesthetic learners (by doing and feeling)

Kinaesthetic learners may learn by being involved in drama or dance as part of the input, handling objects or taking part in ceremonies such as lighting an Advent wreath while an explanation is given. *Walk Thru the Bible* (www.bible.org.uk) is a form of kinaesthetic learning.

Gestures or ritual can help carry meaning for many people. Sermons can create the feelings involved in learning for kinaesthetic learners. Sermons are not necessarily passive.

Below are a few activities that can be used in the church context for communicating information in different ways. They are separated into three groups, but often an activity involves more than one type of learning.

Visual input

- Using banners, art, posters and other images
- Seeing readings (not just listening)
- Using video, an OHP, PowerPoint or flipcharts
- The use of colour (this can be anything from liturgical colour to the use of highlighters on a text)
- Displays
- Looking at artefacts and demonstrations
- Diagrams
- Symbols
- Using description and creating mental images by what is said
- Using activities that spark the imagination

Auditory input

- Giving or listening to talks, sermons, prayers or readings
- Being involved in debates and discussions in groups or pairs

- Using music—for example, prayers and reflections can be spoken over music played quietly. Music can also be used (with or without lyrics) to communicate ideas and feelings
- Using rhythm and rhyme (see page 144)
- Using alliteration and other sound patterns (see page 144)
- Interviews
- Stories
- Using poetry and rap
- Using congregational responses and liturgy
- Using activities that involve listening and talking

Kinaesthetic input

- Taking part in drama, mime, role play, interviews and dance
- Responsive storytelling (where people take part by repeating certain words or actions)
- Handling objects such as a palm cross
- Celebrations—teaching through the way we celebrate—for example, Easter customs, rituals and worship
- Using gestures or movements
- Participation in activities, demonstrations and ritual
- Collecting information in an active way—for example, from posters and other sources around the room
- Handling information—for example, having information on cards and putting it into the order of importance
- Taking part in teaching and learning games—for example, exercises such as matching texts and the situations they relate to
- Taking part in activities that create the emotions of learning

The Quiet Day material in the following worked example uses different types of learning. Read through it and track the different types of learning used.

Reflection on a painting for a Quiet Day

The picture used for the reflection is *Jacob reproaching Laban for giving him Leah in place of Rachel* by Hendrick ter Brugghen. This picture can be seen on the National Gallery website: www.nationalgallery.org.uk. Go to 'Collection', then 'Full Collection Index', then search by the name.

Read Genesis 29. *The Dramatised Bible* (published by Bible Society) can be used if you have one.

Look closely at the painting. Look at the expressions on the faces and the way in which the people hold their bodies. Try to imagine the conversation and what they might be saying to each other. If only this painting could speak! Try some of the following activities:

- Share with the person sitting next to you what you think the people are saying.
- Put your own body in the positions you see in the painting or arrange a group of people into a tableaux of the painting. What do the positions tell you about what they are thinking and feeling?
- Improvise the scene. What are they saying to each other.
- Write in thought and speech bubbles what you think they are saying and thinking.

JACOB

Jacob (in red) had played many tricks on others: we read about them in Genesis 27. But he has just been tricked himself by his uncle Laban (the one sitting down).

Jacob had fallen in love with Laban's youngest daughter, Rachel. He had worked for seven years with no wages so that he could marry her. This was an incredible amount to pay for a wife! Think of your wages or your family wage, and multiply that figure by seven. This gives some indication of Jacob's feelings for Rachel. At the last moment Laban had switched the bride and given Jacob Leah—his elder but not so beautiful daughter. (Brides were heavily veiled in those days and no doubt the wine flowed freely.) Jacob did not notice until it was too late. He had worked for seven years for nothing. What could Jacob do? He had run away from his family. He was on his own with no one to support him.

Look again at Jacob. What would you want to say to him? Share your thoughts with the person next to you.

LABAN

Laban was a man like Jacob—quite capable of cheating others if there was something in it for himself. He is calm, knowing that Jacob can do nothing. He is even working out a scheme to get more money. He offers Jacob Rachel as well as Leah—if Jacob works for another seven years with no wages.

Look again at Laban. How would you describe him as a person? Share your description with the person next to you.

JACOB AND LABAN

The two men fill the front of the painting. This was a society where men dominated. The women had little say in their future. It's a painting about power and lack of it. These two men squabble over the fate of Leah with complete disregard for her.

Look again at the two men. What would you want to say to them? Share your thoughts with the person next to you.

RACHEL

Rachel is in the background, peeping around the wall between the curtains like a little girl. She is in the shadow. All her life she had outshone Leah with her beauty, but not in this painting and not in the Bible story. Jacob loved Rachel passionately and rejected Leah, but God behaved differently. Read Genesis 29:31–35. God knew Leah's worth so he gave her children to love. This is a sign of God's favour in the Bible. God valued Leah when others didn't.

Look again at Rachel. How would you describe her in light of the story? Has the artist got it right? Discuss this in your groups.

LEAH

This is Leah's moment and the light falls on her. She is straight-backed, proud and surrounded with a glow of light. Ter Brugghen has painted her in the same way that other artists painted saints and martyrs. But he does not paint her in a Roman arena facing lions. In his paintings, suffering is silent and undramatic. Leah's martyrdom takes place around the dining-room table. In front of her, the two men who should have cared for her are trying to get rid of her. Her father is trying to give her to Jacob and Jacob is trying to return her like unwanted goods. We cannot begin to imagine what that must have done to Leah's self-esteem. Around her are the broken remains of the food—a bone, a broken roll, scattered crumbs. This is a painting about broken dreams and crushed feelings.

This painting shows no broken Leah, however. Leah stands tall and apart from the sordid bargaining that is going on in front of her. It is literally 'beneath her'. Jacob and her father had always compared her to her sister and she had always come second. The artist reverses this verdict, and so does God. Leah may not be beautiful but you are left in no doubt about the quality of her character. She draws on other sources for self-esteem. She knows her worth, and God, knowing she is unloved by others, shows his love for her by giving her children. She is his child and that is all that matters. This is a painting about power and lack of it. But who has the power? Who lacks it? Leah has a power that comes from within, from God.

Look again at Leah. What would you want to say to her? Write the silent prayer you think Leah might be saying and pin up your prayer around the picture on display if you wish.

We do not often face big dramatic incidents. Despite the news, most of us lead fairly ordinary lives, but that does not mean we do not suffer. Like Leah, our suffering is often undramatic and takes place around the kitchen table, among the people we love, at home. We are often hurt within our close relationships. That is also where we are often healed. The battering we take from life may leave us with low self-esteem, but God values us. His verdict is often different from that of the rest of the world. We are his children; he offers us a relationship with him, a place at his table, a place to be healed.

Prayer time

Invite people to take part in the following reflection, 'A creation of a "table"'. The different parts can be read by different people.

You will need:

- A small table
- A white tablecloth
- A cross
- A bread roll

Two people carry a small table, while others bring a cloth, bread and a cross at appropriate moments in the reading.

This is the table;
the table of martyrdom,
the table of healing.

Two people bring forward a small table.

> *It is the place where we meet every day;*
> *it represents our families;*
> *our friendships.*

Two people cover the table with a cloth.

> *At the table;*
> *in our ordinary relationships,*
> *we are sometimes hurt,*
> *and in turn hurt others.*

Bread is placed on the table.

> *We do not face lions.*
> *We do not enter the arena.*
> *Our arena is everyday life.*

The bread is broken into four pieces.

> *At the table,*
> *in our ordinary relationships*
> *we can be healed*
> *And in turn can heal others.*
> *For you give us unlimited love,*
> *A love we can share with others.*

A cross is placed on the table.

> *Give us strength, Father,*
> *when life knocks our self-esteem,*
> *when we feel undervalued,*
> *when we feel broken.*

Some crumbs are scattered on the cloth.

Remind us that the place where we are hurt,
can also be the place where we are healed.
Hurts that take place in relationships
can be healed in relationships:
with you and with others.

The four pieces of bread are placed in the 'quarters' made by the cross.

Amen

CHAPTER 18

Learners differ in intelligences

Not only do we differ in our degree of intelligence, we may also differ in our type of intelligence. Professor Howard Gardner of Harvard University has made people aware that there may be different types of 'intelligence' (groupings of abilities and skills). Seven of Gardner's 'intelligences' are:

- *Linguistic intelligence:* an ability to understand and use language with its different sounds, rhythms, meanings and moods and the way in which words communicate information.
- *Musical intelligence:* an awareness of the patterns and rhythms in music.
- *Bodily/kinaesthetic intelligence:* the co-ordination of mind, hand and body. Being good at handling objects is a mark of this intelligence.
- *Visual/spatial intelligence:* an ability to create images, a good imagination and an ability to visualize. A good spatial understanding can be a mark of this intelligence.
- *Intrapersonal intelligence:* an ability to think deeply about issues. An awareness of our own thoughts, feelings and behaviour and an ability to reflect on, evaluate and act on them is a mark of this intelligence.
- *Interpersonal intelligence:* the ability to understand others and to relate to them.
- *Logical/mathematical intelligence:* the ability to reason, think logically and use abstract concepts. People with this type of intelligence like order and sequence and enjoy solving problems.

This is not a mandate for pigeon-holing people and saying, 'I (or you) only have one particular type of intelligence.' It is meant to make us aware of diversity and help us to accommodate it. Not all skills and abilities can be used in every session but over a period of time we should try to draw on a range.

WHAT DOES THIS MEAN IN PRACTICE?

The following questions may be helpful in identifying areas of need:

- Are we aware of the different skills and abilities (intelligences) within the church?
- How are skills and abilities identified and fostered?
- Are some people functioning in the wrong areas?
- Are different skills and abilities valued? How is this shown?

Some people assume that 'general intelligence' makes people fit for all areas of service that require thinking. Those who are deemed to be of a high IQ are sometimes given important roles within the church regardless of the *type* of intelligence they have. A brilliant scientist does not always make the best teacher or preacher. We could use Gardner's work to look for variety within the congregation and to match talents to areas of service.

In the following worked example of a youth group session, material drawing on different types of 'intelligences' has been incorporated. Abilities and skills used include:

- Bodily (the first game and the cross activity)
- Visual (the poster and the cross activity)
- Musical (the second game)
- Interpersonal (part of the cross activity and 'working in a group')
- Intrapersonal (part of the cross activity and the worship)
- Mathematical/logical (the 'finding common factors' activity)
- Linguistic (the summary and the text message)

Note: This session has been designed to demonstrate the use of different intelligences. This does not mean that every session you lead should include all seven of the different ways people express their understanding.

'Dying for the world': a youth group session for 11–14s

This is the first in a series on the subject of the cross. The activities are fairly simple, designed to give the group early success and to put them in the frame of mind for tackling some of the more difficult ideas later. Select from the material according to time available.

Aim

The overall aim of the unit is to explore the meaning of the cross using different images.

Objective

The objective for this session is to explore the concept of Christ dying for the world and how that affects us in our daily lives.

INTRODUCTION

Share the objective with the group and then outline the plan for the evening, including the games, Bible exploration, reflective activity and worship.

Play some music from different countries, and have artefacts, pictures and food from around the world in the room. Music from different cultures is available in the 'world music' section of major music shops.

GAMES

Select from these games as time allows, or ask the week before the session which type of game the group would prefer.

Match the food

You will need:

- Food from around the world on numbered plates (make sure no one is allergic to any of it)
- Cards under the plates showing where the food came from
- A globe or large map of the world
- Coloured sticky dots (a different colour for each team)

In teams, people taste the various foods and write down the numbers and where they think each item of food came from. They then have to write the number of each plate on a dot and place it on the correct place on the globe or map.

Match the music

You will need:

- A globe or large map of the world
- Some prizes
- Music from different cultures

Listen to extracts of music from different cultures around the world. The first person to guess correctly where the music comes from has to find the country on the globe or map. Mistakes should be a cause of fun, not embarrassment. The leaders can make their own mistakes!

EXPLORING THE BIBLE

Read John 1:29; John 3:16–17; 1 John 2:2; 2 Corinthians 5:19.

Split into small groups and give each group a photocopy of the passages written out in full. Try the following activities:

- What do the passages all have in common? Ask each group to make a summary of the message of these passages.
- How could this message be put in different words for different purposes and still keep the meaning the same? For example, could it be turned into a text message or a poster? Give each group paper and pens so that they can put their ideas into practice.

The Taizé cross

Outline the story of Taizé to the group.

Brother Roger founded the Taizé community in France during the Second World War. He started by helping people in danger to escape from the Germans. After the war he helped German soldiers who were in prison. This did not make him popular with the local people, but Brother Roger did not divide people up into 'friends' and 'enemies'. He believed that Jesus died for everyone. Over the years, he and the brothers in the community worked tirelessly to bring people of all nationalities together. They travelled to parts of the world where there was war and hatred and tried to bring peace.

Today, people from all over the world come to Taizé, often for a short time, to share in worship and work together. People from different cultures work and pray together and take their deepened understanding of God back to their own country.

The Taizé cross is a way of expressing the gospel message that Christ died for the whole world. The inside of the cross can be filled with faces of people from all over the world.

You will need:

- Glue sticks
- Scissors
- Felt-tipped pens
- Magazines from charities such as Tearfund and Christian Aid, or appropriate secular magazines
- An outline of the Taizé cross on card for each member of the group

Each person also needs to bring a photograph of themselves that they don't mind cutting up.

Place piles of magazines on a table or the floor and give each person an outline of a Taizé cross. Each person cuts out pictures of people of different ages, genders or ethnic groups and adds them to the inside of the cross, keeping within the outline. Leave a space in the middle. In the space a simple cross is drawn with a felt-tipped pen as a reminder of Jesus. Somewhere in the Taizé cross, each person adds his or her own photograph.

It is easy to think about Christ dying for the world and forgetting just what that means.

- It means that Christ died for us: that is why our face is on the cross.
- It means that Christ died for the people we care for and who care for us: if you want to, add some names to the back of the cross.
- It means that Christ died for the people we don't like: you don't need to add their names, but do spend a few moments thinking of them.
- It means that Christ died for the people where you live: write the name of your town or village on the back of the cross.
- It means that Christ died for the people in this country: write the country where you live on the back of the cross.

- It means that Christ died for the people in other countries: look at the faces on your cross.

We may not be able to find all the countries represented on our cross on the map, but God can. It's hard to imagine loving a world; sometimes it's easier to imagine God loving individuals. Over six billion individuals live in the world.

Note: The above activity draws on material from *A-cross the World* by Martyn Payne and Betty Pedley, published by BRF.

What difference does it make on Monday morning?

Knowing that Christ died for the world, including us, means we can face life realizing we are loved to an extent that is difficult to imagine. It also affects how we treat others. No one is worthless. If Christ thought they were worth dying for, then we should treat them with respect. That does not mean letting other people treat us badly, for we too were worth dying for. We too should be treated with respect. Being a Christian is not being a doormat!

WORSHIP

Invite the group to sit in a circle around a globe. Place some tealight candles in saucers of water or damp sand, and arrange them around the globe. Turn out the lights.

Use some Taizé music and songs to set a worshipful atmosphere, or sing the following songs:

- What kind of love is this?
- There is a redeemer

Ask people to look at their crosses and together pray for the different groups that the cross represents—our world, country, town, those we don't like, those we love, ourselves. Use the words and images on the cross as a guide.

Prayer

This prayer can be read out. People can join in the bold line if this is appropriate for your group.

Thank you, God, that you so loved the world that you sent your son,
and you so loved me.
Thank you, Lord, that you died for the world,
and for me.
Thank you for caring for those I love and those I don't
and for being a God who can embrace the whole world,
and me.
Amen

CHAPTER 19

We differ in concentration spans

Some of us can concentrate for long periods of time, others can't. There are a number of factors that affect concentration spans:

- Age and personality
- Context: church, home, individual or group
- Content: interesting, boring or relevant
- Type of learning: sermon, study, activity or discussion
- Motivation and purpose
- Emotional factors
- Time of day

Some of us can concentrate on a computer game for an hour, but our concentration drifts in a 20-minute sermon. Worry, lack of motivation and the degree of difficulty affect concentration. Difficult material may need to be taught in a series of short sessions. The way material is presented can also increase the length of time we can attend to a subject.

WHAT DOES THIS MEAN IN PRACTICE?

Bear concentration spans in mind, particularly when taking children's talks and Sunday club sessions. Break up long teaching sessions. Look through commercially produced Sunday club material and make sure that the youth group sessions provide breaks that create smaller units of appropriate length.

Long sessions on difficult material *may* need breaking up, even for adults. Several short inputs are sometimes better than one long one. It is better to do a small amount well rather than attempt a large amount and have much of it forgotten. Below are some of the ways a session can be broken up. Select appropriately from these suggestions.

- Do an activity that allows people to get up and move around for a few moments.
- Change the type of activity.
- Stop for refreshments.
- Break for group work or discussion.
- Give people a few minutes (in pairs or groups) to come up with a way of memorizing what they have learned and how it could be applied.
- In pairs, invite people to create questions to ask about what has been learned.
- Have a music or worship break.

Note: This does not mean that all sessions should be broken up. It would be inappropriate to break a session if it is going well and people are captivated.

'Who am I?': a children's talk

You will need:

- Large strips of paper, slit as in the diagram on page 167
- A large felt-tipped pen
- A baby bracelet of the type used in hospitals, or a paper equivalent (see instructions on page 167)
- Lots of paper bracelets and pens scattered about the church
- A large paper hand and pens at the back of the church

WHO AM I?

'I am' are important words. I am (*give your name*). Who are you?

(*Ask various children to come up and say who they are, starting with the words 'I am'.*)

It's important to know who we are. If we are born in a hospital, a tiny plastic bracelet is put around our wrists to show who we are and to whom we belong.

(*Show a baby bracelet and read the name on it.*)

I've made a bigger version.

(*Produce paper/card strip. Ask for a volunteer to wear a bracelet. This can be either an adult or a child, but do choose your volunteer with care.*)

Write the name of the volunteer on the bracelet and join it into a circle on their arm. If appropriate, you could ask one of the children who came to the front initially to help you do this. It doesn't matter if the bracelet is loose: the volunteer can bend his or her arm to keep it in place.)

Knowing who we are involves more than knowing our name. We need to know who we belong to, who cares for us.

(Ask the volunteer who he or she belongs to—make sure you have chosen your volunteer with care. Use one strip of paper or card for every person that they mention, adding the bracelets to arms and legs. For example, write 'Dan belongs to his mum'; 'Dan belongs to his brother'; 'Dan belongs to his nan'; 'Dan belongs to his grandad', and so on. Ask the children present to help you put the bracelets on the volunteer.)

We have covered (volunteer's name) with bracelets, but he doesn't really need them. He is not likely to forget. If he got lost he would not need a bracelet to remind him who he is and where he belongs.

(Ask your volunteer what he or she would do or say if lost.)

Sometimes we write a note on our hands to remind ourselves of something important.

(Do this using face crayons or lipstick, and say that you are using special crayons that write on the skin.)

In the Bible it says that God writes our names on the palms of his hands—because we are his. We can find this verse in Isaiah 49:16. We do not only belong to our families; we belong to God.

(Read 2 Corinthians 6:16b.)

When someone asks me who I am, I can say:

- I am (*give your name*).
- I am the daughter of (*give your parents' names*).
- I am God's child.

The Bible does not mean that God literally has hands covered with writing. It's a 'word picture'—a way of saying that we belong to God and he never forgets us because we are important to him. We are his children, even when we are grown up.

On the seats are lots of bracelets and pens. If you want to write your name on a bracelet, or anything important that struck you during the service, you can do that now and then put the bracelet on. Adults are welcome to do this too, and can also help the children with their bracelets.

(*Leave a few minutes for people to make bracelets if they wish. Add an extra bracelet to the volunteer, saying 'Dan belongs to God'.*)

When you wake up on Monday morning you can say:

- I am... add your name.
- I belong to... say the names of the members of your family.
- I belong to God and I am important to him.
- I am his child and he never forgets me.

Perhaps you could take a few extra minutes in bed to say your name out loud and to remember that God has your name 'written on the palm of his hand'.

While we pray I want you to hold one hand open flat. With one finger of the other hand, draw the first letter of your name on the palm of your flat hand. Just keep drawing that letter while I say the prayer.

(*Demonstrate drawing the letter. Adults can help young children with this.*)

Thank you, God, that we know who we are and where we belong. We belong to those who love us—we belong to you. Never let us forget that you have written our names on the palm of your hand; we are yours. Amen.

At the back of the church is a giant paper hand. It reminds us of the word picture from the Bible: 'God has written our names on the palm of his hand.'

If you wish to, you can write your name on the hand as a way of reminding yourself that God never forgets you.

Note: The reference to 'walls' in Isaiah 49:16 (NIV) is to the city of Zion and refers to the people as well as the city.

Paper bracelets

You will need:

- Sheets of A4 paper in a variety of colours
- Ruler
- Scissors
- Pencil

Mark the short sides of each A4 sheet of paper at 3cm intervals. Join the corresponding marks to make strips along the length of the sheet. Cut the strips along the pencil lines. (Each A4 sheet will make seven bracelets.)

Mark 3cm in from each end of the bracelet. Cut slits to halfway across the bracelet, one on each side as shown. Join the bracelet by interlocking the slits.

3cm

3cm

SECTION SIX

Remembering what we have learned

CHAPTER 20

Remembering what we learn

We can remember things consciously and in other ways, but we do not remember everything that we have learned. Our brains would have trouble coping if we did, so we are designed to forget some things to prevent overload. Our memories are both complex and imperfect. We also tend to remember the beginning and end of a session, but attention often slips in the middle.

One way of thinking about the memory is to think in terms of an everyday working memory and a long-term memory. Our working memory includes our short-term memory, where we store information for a short time. Working memory is what we use for moment-by-moment decisions. Working memory also acts as a 'gatekeeper', letting some things in and keeping others out. We particularly remember what we pay conscious attention to, and factors such as our emotions, beliefs and the context focus our conscious attention.

Long-term memory is different, involving the release of chemicals that act as 'fixatives'. Part of the brain, called the 'amygdala', decides the emotional value of information. If the information is emotionally significant, it is packaged and stored.

Memory is all about connections. When learning takes place, a connection is made and a pathway is created between brain cells (imagine them touching hands to form a long line). Signals, electrical and chemical, are sent down the pathway. The more signals that are sent down the pathway, the more it is strengthened and the more information is remembered. To use another analogy, it's like walking a footpath: the more often it is walked, the more likely it is to remain open as a permanent pathway.

WHAT DOES THIS MEAN IN PRACTICE?

How a teaching session starts and ends is important (preachers have always known this). Begin and end in style. Unusual beginnings capture attention and should make us want to listen. To stop attention drifting in the middle, we may need to create several small beginnings by having different sections. This also helps to break up longer sessions.

We shouldn't waste the precious moments at the end of a sermon. End with a phrase that will sink deep within and cause reflection. Use the end of a teaching session to summarize what has been learned.

Relating teaching to emotions, beliefs and real-life situations helps with retention. If learning is to be remembered and transferred into our long-term memory, it needs to have personal significance, be emotionally 'charged' or have relevance for us.

Going back over what has been learned just once, even if it is only a few key points, makes a difference. Try some of the following.

- Put summaries on the screen or flipchart at the end of a Bible study.
- Sum up at the end of a talk (if appropriate).
- Ask people to share with the person next to them something they have learned (always warn people that you are going to do this).

The following sermon starts and ends in a way that people will probably notice. Look through the middle section; will it still maintain interest? Does it have personal value and significance? Is it likely to touch emotions and be remembered?

'The people who do': a sample sermon on 1 Samuel 24 and Luke 14:15-24

So far I have not murdered anybody. I have also resisted stealing, committing adultery and perjury—but it is still only 10.30 in the morning. I'm working on covetousness—that's a very nice top you're wearing, Kirsten.

The story of David and Saul in the cave is a story of what David didn't do. Saul, the king, was hunting David—the boy wonder; the slayer of Goliath. Saul was sick to death of David and was suffering from a bad case of jealousy with a lot of paranoia thrown in. He was determined to get rid of David. Saul sent David on dangerous missions but the wretched boy refused to die. He tried throwing his spear at him (twice) but he missed each time, so Saul took to hunting him down personally.

David and his men were hiding at the back of a deep cave. Saul stopped to relieve himself in the cave, little knowing that his enemy was there. David's men urged him to kill Saul while he had the chance, but David refused. Instead, he crept up and cut a piece off Saul's cloak while Saul was otherwise engaged. Having done this, David followed Saul out of the cave and told him that he could have killed him but didn't. So David became famous for what he didn't do. And you have to admire him. Most people would have felt that Saul had it coming.

In our second reading, Jesus asks us to do much, much more than refrain from doing harm. It is very easy to list the things we don't do and feel quite righteous about it. The popular media image of Christian living is often negative. Christians are seen as people who:

- don't gamble
- don't smoke
- don't swear
- don't drink
- don't sleep around
- don't have much fun

It is easy to imagine a Christian arriving at the gates of heaven with a list of all the things they haven't done. There are various reasons for this. One is that it is easier to say what you don't do than what you do. But, personally, I don't want the words 'She never did anyone any harm' on my tombstone. Would it not be better to have done some good?

Another reason for being known for what we don't do is the fear of being called a 'do-gooder' if we do something positive. This little phrase does a lot to deter people from doing good. It is said with a sneer. It is a label that no one wants. But what does it actually mean someone who does good? What are the alternatives? A 'do-badder'? A 'do-nothing-at-aller'? This sarcastic little label often prevents people from doing something positive.

So a picture is built up of Christians as a negative group of people who have little fun. Nothing could be further from the attitude of Jesus.

First of all, this story in Luke's Gospel is about a party—there are lots of parties in the Bible. Celebration definitely gets the divine stamp of approval. Jesus was into parties. He often likened heaven to one. Luke tells us what he says to one host in the preceding passage, Luke 14:12–14. He tells the host to stop inviting all the important and influential people and open the party to the riff-raff. I bet that was a conversation stopper.

I don't know if you ever buy celebrity magazines. I sometimes pick them up at the dentist's and they absolutely fascinate me. They are full of people being photographed arriving at parties looking lovely. I suspect that some of the dresses cost more than my entire year's wages and I spend most of my time muttering, 'I wouldn't be seen dead in that' and 'Haven't they heard of Marks and Spencer's?'

To me, the world of glossy magazines is another planet. It is a world where the main aim of life is to be seen at the right parties with the right people, wearing the right clothes.

Jesus doesn't see it quite like that. At the party we call heaven, the people to be seen with are those who are poor, the rejected people of society, the underdogs. These are the people to be seen with as far as God is concerned.

In Jesus' parable, the important people have been invited to the party. All cry off, even though they have had the date in their diaries for ages, and the excuses are pathetic:

- 'I have to inspect some land.' Why? Is it going somewhere? Has it got a sell-by date? It will still be there tomorrow.
- 'I have just bought two oxen.' Give the oxen a day off, they won't mind.
- 'I've just got married.' So what? It's not an infectious disease that puts you in quarantine! Marriage doesn't usually take people by surprise; you can give your excuses early.

So the host throws the party open to the people living on the street and in the alleys of the town. He does not get excuses from them. People who are disadvantaged through no fault of their own accept his invitation, for they know they are needy. The rich and influential in this story do not see themselves as needy. They have better things to do than go to D-list parties:

- They did not know that they were blind to the important things in life.
- They did not know that they were poor in spirit.

But no amount of wealth and influence could disguise these facts.

There is nothing inherently wrong with wealth or influence. It is only wrong when it lulls us into forgetting our need for God—when it stops us saying 'Yes' to God's invitation to come to the party.

This story in Luke is a very positive parable. The image is

positive—a party. God's kingdom and heaven are both likened to parties. Yet sometimes we feel that parties aren't quite appropriate for the Bible. Better to stick with hymn singing—it sounds more holy!

God thinks differently. He is lavish with his feast; he throws the doors open wide so that all can come.

(Arrange to have some members of the congregation release balloons, party poppers and so on at this point.)

God calls us to do something positive—to share our lives with people in need, to invite everybody into his kingdom. He does not just ask us to avoid doing the *wrong* thing; he asks us to do the *right* thing.

If we live in the light of this parable, we just might become known as people who do, not people who don't.

CHAPTER 21

Improving our memories

There are different ways of remembering; all have their advantages and disadvantages. Usually we employ a number of tactics when we memorize.

Focusing on the content

This works by repeating things, making patterns and lists and using memory tricks (mnemonics). For example, 'Richard Of York Gave Battle In Vain' is a mnemonic for the colours of the rainbow. Practice and repetition are crucial for this type of memorizing.

Focusing on the senses

This method works by linking content with the senses (touch, smell, sight, sound and taste). Generally speaking, the more our senses are used, the more we will remember. Try some of the following.

- Associate what is learned with something that will appeal to the senses—a scene or image, a sound, a taste, a texture or a smell.
- Say or explain things out loud while walking about or running a finger across the words (this is called 'pole-bridging').
- Use music, rhythm and rhyme to help with memorizing: sing information to a well-known tune.
- Use the imagination and 'inner eye' to picture the material and fix it in the memory.

Focusing on the context

This means linking what we have learned with a particular context. Memories are often recalled by the circumstances surrounding them and the context. For example, a piece of music that was playing when we learned something can trigger the memory. The police use this type of memory in crime reconstructions.

When we want to remember something, we can give it significance (asking, 'Why am I remembering this?') or file it in the mind by:

- visualising it
- making it personal
- exaggerating it
- connecting it with something else
- sharing it with someone else

Then practise recalling it.

WHAT DOES THIS MEAN IN PRACTICE?

The sermon has been criticized as a passive experience that does not engage people—an experience that most people forget. This does not have to be so. As long as we bear in mind how people remember information, what we said can be retained. When preparing a talk, a sermon or a group session, select from some of the following ways of encouraging retention according to the context.

- Use repetition and mnemonics.
- Use gesture and body language.
- Use descriptions of scenes that will engage the senses. The brain is a powerful organ, and imagining tastes and feels can stimulate us to recreate the experience in our minds.
- Use acronyms, alliteration, rhythm and other sound patterns.

- Create a learning context: we need to pay careful attention to the atmosphere in which teaching occurs.
- Look after relationships, for that is where we learn best. Respect for the person preaching or teaching grows out of a wider relationship, and that increases our ability to learn. Learning in relationship does not necessarily mean group work; it means building good relationships that make people willing to learn from each other.
- Engage the senses as appropriate when presenting material. What is appropriate to a youth group session may not be appropriate to a sermon.

One fact about memory that needs to be borne in mind is that most of what is taught is remembered—by the teacher. If we want people to remember, we need to encourage them to teach (that is, those who want to do it and have the gift). Even preparing a small amount to present to others often fixes it in our minds.

'The annunciation': reflective material for a Quiet Day

This material uses the painting of the annunciation by Duccio. This picture can be seen on the National Gallery website: www.nationalgallery.org.uk. Go to 'Collection', then 'Full Collection Index', then search by name.

You will need:

- Printed copies of the painting, or the painting reproduced on an OHP or PowerPoint
- A Polaroid or digital camera
- A selection of reflective music
- Pens
- Paper
- Photographs of the participants as teenagers (arrange for participants to bring these photos with them)
- Photocopies of the carol 'The angel Gabriel from heaven came' from *The Shorter New Oxford Book of Carols* (OUP)

Note: check church copyright over images and music.

A number of strategies are employed in this Quiet Day material to help people remember it. They include use of the senses, drawing conscious attention to things and creating a context. Participants are encouraged to visualize and share. At the end of the day, the participants are invited to reflect on what they have learned and immediately use it to produce a 'signed' carol. Emotional value and personal relevance have also been built in to make the material easier to remember.

Objective

To explore Mary's reaction to the angel Gabriel's message and what we can learn from that about our own reactions to God's will.

USING THE BIBLE

Ask one of the participants to read Luke 1:26–38 and Matthew 1:18–25.

LOOKING AT THE PAINTING

Look at the painting. Notice the body language of the angel and Mary. What is the body language telling us?

ACTIVITY

Invite two people to come and create the tableau depicted in the painting. Use a Polaroid or digital camera to take a picture.

USING THE BIBLE

Read Luke 1:26–33.

LOOKING AT THE PAINTING

In the painting, the angel strides towards Mary, his hand outstretched and carrying a baton, which is a symbol of authority. Mary steps backwards, seemingly in retreat. But behind her is a wall. She is potentially cornered. Does she accept what this angel brings, or does she continue to retreat? If the latter, ask yourself, where can we retreat when an angel of God stands before us? Mary has a choice: saying 'yes' is costly, but so is saying, 'no'. Was the artist right to draw Mary backing away? Share your ideas with a neighbour.

ACTIVITY

Spend a few moments in reflection while music plays. Ask people to think of a time when it was difficult to either say 'yes' or 'no' to God because both had important consequences.

USING THE BIBLE

Read Luke 1:34–38.

LOOKING AT THE PAINTING

Look again at the painting. Notice the open door—a symbol of being open to God. Mary is hesitant, but she opens the door to God. There are times when we fling open the door. There are times when we close it fast shut. There are times when we open it a crack, wary of what we are letting ourselves in for.

ACTIVITY

On the sheets of paper, invite participants to draw how their 'door' looks at the moment. Encourage people to be honest. No one else will see their work. When everyone has drawn their door, spend a few moments reflecting on what causes the door to be as open or closed as it is. Encourage people to be honest with God. If we want to be more open to God, we will need his help.

USING THE BIBLE

Read Matthew 1:18–25.

LOOKING AT THE PAINTING

Now look at Mary again. How old do you think she is? Mary was probably a teenager. The marriageable age for girls was about 13, with a year for betrothal. Mary could have been about 14. Think of the dreams for the future she would have had—largely centred on home and family in those days.

ACTIVITY

Look at the photographs that participants have brought of themselves as teenagers. Share them with each other and, if appropriate, what their individual teenage dreams were. Encourage people to feel relaxed about laughing—fashions and hairstyles have changed!

Think how the angel's message interrupted Mary's dreams. Having a child before she was married would have carried the death penalty if Jewish law had been applied. As it was, Mary would have suffered disgrace and no man would have married her. Joseph intended to divorce her—until God intervened. At the moment recorded in the painting, Mary did not know that Joseph would stand by her. She probably assumed divorce and a lifetime of loneliness and isolation from society. Perhaps she was busy burying her dreams. She had to let her dreams go in order to embrace God's new future for her.

We all have to let go of our dreams sometimes. Sometimes our dreams are unrealistic or ill-advised, or do not come to fruition when our lives take a different direction. But we can find God in our lives whatever direction they take. Sometimes God asks us to let go of one dream in order to embrace another. If Mary had not let go of her dreams, we would never have heard of this peasant girl from Nazareth.

❖

Spend a few moments thinking back on life. Invite people to remember themselves as young men or women. Encourage them to visualize themselves growing up, through the different stages of life. Reflect on the fact that Mary was just an ordinary teenager of her time—just as we were of ours—when God chose her. Think of the times when we may have let something go, just as Mary did, in order to embrace God's future for us. It may have been something small; it may have been something big. Only God and we know. It is between us two. Just remember, he is on our side. He wants what is best for us.

CONCLUDING THE REFLECTION

Invite people to reflect on what they have learned from the Bible readings and the painting. In twos or threes, share anything that has been learned from the day and what participants will take away with them. Refer back to the objective.

ACTIVITY

Invite people to spend a few minutes in their small groups and then report back.

Give out photocopies of the carol 'The angel Gabriel from heaven came' from *The Shorter New Oxford Book of Carols* (OUP). Before singing the carol, go over the words and the music together to ensure everyone is familiar with the words and the tune.

As a group, create some signs for each line (like a signing choir of the hearing-impaired). Do this by using what has been learned and expressing insights through the signs and the music. (Those who don't wish to sign can just contribute to the discussion and join in with the singing.)

Practise singing the carol and signing as agreed by the group. Finally, perform the carol together.

'The annunciation': a dramatic version

As an alternative to the signed carol, some people may like to practise and perform the story as a drama, perhaps using the suggestion below.

Cast: three people standing in a line. The first wears a label saying 'God'. The second wears a label saying 'Gabriel'. The third wears a label saying 'Mary'.

The lines are repeated in turn with appropriate gestures and expressions

God   I sent.
Gabriel   I went.
Mary   I was surprised.

God   I chose her.
Gabriel   I approached her.
Mary   I backed away.

God   I watched.
Gabriel   I spoke.
Mary   I listened.

God   I trusted.
Gabriel   I wondered.
Mary   I struggled.

God	I waited.
Gabriel	I heard.
Mary	I said 'yes'.

God	I rejoiced.
Gabriel	I returned.
Mary	I made ready.

God	My trust was repaid.
Gabriel	My fears were put aside.
Mary	My life was turned upside down.

God	My joy was complete.
Gabriel	My work was finished.
Mary	My work had begun.

Final prayer

End the Quiet Day with a prayer.

> **Father, you chose a young girl from Nazareth:**
> **not much education,**
> **not much status,**
> **an ordinary girl.**
> **You gave her a choice,**
> **a hard choice,**
> **but she decided to open the door and let you in.**
> **You turned her life upside down,**
> **and you gave her a new future:**
> **it was not without pain,**
> **it was not without suffering,**
> **but it was worthwhile.**
> **Give us the courage to keep the door open**
> **and let you in.**
> **Amen**

Moving on

CHAPTER 22

Coping with change and handling discussions

Real learning is about change, and change can be painful. When faced with change or thinking about implementing change, it might be helpful to think through the following ideas (which draw on *The Survivor's Guide to Church Life* by James and Nina Rye, IVP).
Here are some questions to ask ourselves:

- Is this change necessary or is it change for change's sake?
- Is this change important?
- Is this change biblical?
- Has change been arrived at prayerfully?
- What do other churches do?

DISTINGUISHING BETWEEN 'WRONG' AND 'DIFFERENT'

Sometimes we dislike change because the familiar has suddenly become different (try changing the tune to a much-loved hymn). Difference is sometimes the result of one person or group being wrong and another right. At other times it is just a matter of facing the fact that there are other ways of doing things. Variety is God-given; difference in itself is not wrong.

DISTINGUISHING THE DIFFERENCE BETWEEN SELF-CENTRED AND GOD-CENTRED CHANGE

Self-interest is something that does have to be faced when dealing with change. We need to ask ourselves the following questions:

- Is this change (or resistance to change) a means of getting our own way?
- Is this change (or opposition) a way of getting us noticed, or is it God-centred?
- Is this change (or resistance) about vested interests, status or power rather than the issue in question?
- Is the desire to keep things the same a sign that we are not admitting past mistakes?
- Is our opposition to change a manifestation of our reluctance to grow?

USE OF LANGUAGE

We need to watch our language when dealing with change. It is better to say something like, 'I find 'X' hard to accept' or 'I feel that what you say might take us in the wrong direction' than, 'What you are suggesting is wrong.' The first two show the humility to leave open the possibility that we might have misunderstood or that our emotions might be getting in the way.

THEOLOGICAL AND PERSONALITY FACTORS

We sometimes defend our lack of desire for change as a reflection of an unchanging God. We are not God! We still have some changing to do in order to become more like him. In order to grow into his likeness, we may have to change our attitudes and our behaviour.

Personality factors also affect change. Some of us thrive on change; others are naturally cautious about new ventures. Some of us have lives full of change and, as a result, welcome the stability of church; others are unaccustomed to change in their lives and carry that expectation into church life.

ATTITUDES

We should hold on to our understanding of the truth with humility. Our understanding of the Bible and God's will is not perfect. We need to check the changes we want to introduce, or our resistance to change, with wise and trusted fellow Christians. We need to learn to listen and to be patient.

It is also helpful to remember that being right is not enough: how we implement change or defend the status quo matters, and the ends do not justify the means. Out of respect for others, we sometimes need to limit our freedom. In turn, however, others should not use their reluctance to change to dominate the church. We should try to identify with each other's position and understand that there is often a genuine fear of where change will lead, and an equally genuine fear of where a refusal to change may leave the church.

PLANNING FOR CHANGE

We need to plan for change and warn people that change will be taking place. Do not just spring change on your unsuspecting group. We need to work together to ensure that everyone understands what will happen and why. We need to decide what pace is right for each situation, thinking through the short- and long-term implications for the church as well as for ourselves and other individuals involved. We often need time to get used to ideas. We sometimes need to hear things regularly restated so that they cease to feel 'new'.

USING THE RIGHT CHANNELS AND METHODS

Sabotage is not an acceptable Christian tactic for stopping change; neither is bullying or intimidation an appropriate way of implementing change. We need to be aware of the subtle ways that sabotage, bullying and intimidation can creep into the life of the church—often unconsciously.

HANDLING DISCUSSIONS

Many of the points mentioned above also apply to running discussions, for that is where difference of opinion often emerges. However, it is also worth noting that:

- We should not interrupt each other.
- One or two people should not be allowed to dominate a discussion. It is possible to stop a few people dominating the discussion by breaking groups into pairs or threes, so that the dominant minority cannot overwhelm the whole group.
- We should speak respectfully to each other even if we disagree.
- We should constantly remind each other that we are brothers and sisters in Christ.
- We should affirm contributions wherever possible.
- We should allow that there may be more than one answer or option.
- We should create an atmosphere that opens up discussion rather than closing it down.
- We should be honest without becoming ruthless.

We
fact
eve
stra
nee
thin
thro
intr

Mak

- Pu
  re
- Pu
  or
  (Y
- Pu
  im
  do
- Pu
  ac

In six
anoth